WORDS
OF
REVOLUTION

TOM SKINNER

WORDS OF REVOLUTION

A call to involvement in the REAL revolution

Zondervan Publishing House
Grand Rapids

Contents

Preface

When I was asked to come to Chicago and share something of my background, experiences and ideas, I had no idea what would happen. I was committed to telling the truth about racism, poverty, violence, and corruption as I had seen and experienced them.

Ask anyone from the street, man. He's an expert on any of these subjects. You won't "jive" him with double talk about your programs of social, economic or political progress. *He knows.* And I know. I've been there. I was born in Harlem and have lived out my life where exploitation, oppression and violence are a way of life.

To a great many people, the "great American dream" is a nightmare.

Everywhere I go I hear people say, "The system's got to go, man," and "We gotta do away with the system." People are fed up. Blacks and whites are sick of the hypocrisy and corruption. Young people are fed up with the world their parents are handing them. Poor and middle-class citizens are reacting to the inequities they see in society.

In short, there are many people eager for change. And in my experience, and in my opinion, *revolution in America is inevitable.* It's not a matter, any more, of race. It's not just the blacks, the poor or the young who are protesting. The call for revolution comes from many different corners of our society and various levels of our culture.

This was the message I took to Chicago.

Chicago is a great city and has given the world much to be proud of. But there is the other side — the side that makes the headlines.

When I arrived, some revolutionaries had just left Chicago. The so-called Conspiracy Seven trial had recently ended. A weathermen faction of the SDS had gone on a destructive rampage. The trial of anti-war demonstrators charged with destroying a draft board office was news. Charges and counter-charges regarding the raid and subsequent shooting of Black Panther leaders were flying back and forth.

But you know, Chicago isn't really so different.

The same headlines — even with some of the same names — make news in Detroit, San Francisco, New York and Los Angeles. Chicago is just a microcosm of the unrest, violence and attitudes that are rocking the rest of America.

No one city has a corner on frustrated poor people, oppressed black people, disenchanted young people or hypocritical older types.

What I saw in Chicago I have seen in Harlem, Mobile, Berkeley, or Minneapolis.

I went into the high schools and rapped with the kids. I went into the streets and spent hours talking with gang members, poor people, addicts and prostitutes. I know, man, *I know* their problems. And I understand the feelings of the average man trying to make a go of life.

I suppose my notoriety as a gang leader got me on the radio and TV shows while I was in Chicago. People listened anyway.

But the climax of my visit to Chicago has to be the series of giant rallies we had in the Chicago Colosseum. It was a peaceful setting, so we didn't get many headlines, but I was amazed and glad to see fantastic crowds fill that huge stadium every night for a week.

It was here I shared with those who came the ideas of this book. I talked about revolution, about radical change for America. And I was thrilled to see literally hundreds of people, each night, commit themselves to this Cause.

We didn't pull any punches. Maybe that's why this book,

Words of Revolution, will be considered bad medicine by a lot of people.

But I'm convinced America is at her crisis hour. *Revolution is inevitable.* It's just a matter of which faction is going to prove strongest and will win out in the end. I believe most Americans are so apathetic that they will just sit back and go to whoever wins the struggle.

A few of us are convinced that revolution has to happen in America. Where we disagree with other radicals is in how to achieve it — and what you are going to do when you do away with the old system.

We touch on all the "gutsy" issues, the emotionally explosive topics. We step on a lot of toes. We have our own ideas about changing the system, about toppling the corrupt, racist and oppressive elements of the system.

Yes, I am a radical. I am committed to revolution. I am committed to doing something about the suffering, shame, and misery in America.

And I'm finding allies in my Cause. I believe it is my mission to channel this radical, revolutionary spirit into a positive program of change — the *only* program that will work for all people.

I want to gain the confidence and support of those — especially among the young — who have "dropped out," "tripped out" or "copped out" on society.

Instead of frustration, despair, disenchantment, apathy or hopelessness, I believe I have discovered a powerful positive plan for confronting the system.

These eight chapters comprise such a strategy. If you will approach this book with an open-minded attitude, you will discover the radical, life-changing content of these chapters.

We might even motivate *you* to go out with *Words of Revolution.*

TOM SKINNER

Brooklyn, N.Y.

Introduction

This is the rationale for my new book, *Words of Revolution*:

I am deeply impressed as I read both the Major and Minor Prophets of the Old Testament that their preaching and their messages were effective because they spoke to the issues of their day. They scratched where people itched. They answered questions that people were asking, and all the time it was "Thus saith the Lord," always relevant, always effective, always to the point.

I'm convinced that if the message of Jesus Christ is to have intellectual integrity and validity for our time, it must speak to the issues. Our time has been described as an age of revolution, and there is no doubt when historians come to document our day they will call it, "The Time of Revolution." Tremendous gaps separate the haves from the have nots, the rich from the poor, black from white, young from old, labor from management. The young, the black, the poor, labor, the have-nots, are now in open rebellion and revolution against the established institutions of our time. Obviously, all sides need to have a clear directive from God, as to which way we should go.

Words of Revolution seeks to speak to all sides of the issues from God's point of view. While there are many on all sides of the argument who will disagree with the philosophy of this book, few will be able to argue that it is not Biblically based.

Words of Revolution seeks to separate the myth surrounding Jesus Christ from Jesus Christ as a person. Jesus Christ is not a church or an institution; He is a person. He is not a democrat or a republican, He is the Lord of heaven and earth. He is not a capitalist or a communist, He's the Christ of God. He's not black or white, He is God's answer to the entire human dilemma. Therefore, if He is going to be worshiped, He must be worshiped as the Lord of heaven and earth.

There are those on the right who seek to force Jesus Christ as the head of the status quo, the maintainer of the existing system. He is not. There are those on the left who try to picture Him as a militant, seeking to use Him as the leader of every revolutionary cause. He is not.

In the revolution that Jesus Christ has come to establish, Jesus Christ doesn't take sides, He takes over.

Words of Revolution has been written to help focus the attention of the evangelical world on the type of preaching that must be done, especially in the urban centers of our country, where the problems are so enormous and unique.

Words of Revolution was written also to speak to the hearts of the radical young people of our time who have written-off Jesus Christ as being irrelevant, or "sissy," or white-anglo-saxon-middle-class-protestant-republican maintaining the existing status quo. It was written to clarify for them that Jesus Christ is, rather, a "gutsy" contemporary, a radical revolutionary. In essence, it was written to say to them, that if you are looking for a revolutionary leader, Jesus Christ, is where it's at.

Words of Revolution was written for an overwhelming number of black people who have given up on Christianity as a "white man's religion," passed off on black people to keep them in their place. It was written for young militant blacks who have identified the message of Jesus Christ with the old order, and who feel that in the coming black revolution all that belongs to the old order must go, including the message of Christ. It was written for many black clergymen who are searching for a sound Biblical theology in the midst of the black revolution.

Words of Revolution was written to the establishment — to say to them that much of what the young, the black, the have-nots or the poor are saying, is not all being said by a bunch of long-haired, militant, bizarre insurrectionists and anarchists; but much of what is said is being said from a frustrated generation of people who see so many flaws, so much sin, hypocrisy and immorality in the establishment.

Words of Revolution also prophesies to the establishment and says to it, that if its system is not built upon Jesus Christ it is "weighed in the balances and found wanting" and it too will reach the judgment of God.

In essence, *Words of Revolution* says that God has pronounced judgment on all the systems of men, and that in the midst of all of the revolutions that are going on God has a revolution of His own. God is building His own kingdom, His own system, and it begins through a personal transformation when man recognizes the utter depravity of his own nature and the only possibility of the annihilation of that depravity and the replacement of it with the resurrected life of Jesus Christ, which is offered through His death and shed blood.

Second Corinthians 5:17 — Therefore if any man be in Christ, he is a new creation; old things are passed away; and behold, all things are become new — is the basis of real revolution. A revolution is defined as taking an existing situation which is proved to be unworkable, archaic, impracticable, out-of-date, tearing it down, destroying it, and replacing it with a system that works. That in essence is what Jesus Christ came to do. Jesus Christ said that the human nature is archaic, impracticable, out-of-date. He is come to destroy it, by His death on the cross, to forgive the results of human nature, by His shed blood, and to establish a new man, which ultimately brings about a new revolution by His resurrection.

Words of Revolution was written to say, that there is only one man who ever walked the face of the earth the way that God intended man to live. There is only one man who was a true revolutionary. There is only one man who can truly change man's corrupt systems. There is only one man who can balance the scale of injustice, hunger, poverty, racism, hate, war, and division. There is only one man who has the unique ability to be all things to all men. There is only one man who can give us the authority to be what God intended us to be. There is only one man who can motivate us to real and proper ambitions. There is only one man who can help us to truly be the Church. He is the Lord from heaven, Jesus Christ, God's Son.

In essence, *Words of Revolution,* points to God's Son.

WORDS
OF
REVOLUTION

1

Take Two Revolutionaries . . .

I think one of the most important questions that has been asked of me is: "Tom Skinner, what do you have to say that is any different? There has been a lot of rhetoric, a lot of speeches, and a lot of noise about the issues and problems of the world. Why do you think that you have anything different to say than anyone else?"

There are many who make no bones about claiming that the church, religion, the Bible have not worked for them. In fact, to many these three forces are full of phoniness. "Religion hasn't worked, it hasn't solved any problems," they say. Still others point the finger at hypocrites who claim to be Christians, preachers who don't really mean business, and church people who are not really sincere.

These are valid questions. Why should you listen to me among all those who discuss the issues of our times? And why do I talk about Jesus Christ? Who is Jesus Christ? Who is God? What is the Bible? And what is it about all these that should make you want to listen?

In this hour when there is so much conflict, anarchistic revolution, bigotry, disturbance and war . . . when there is poverty, hunger, and hate, what does God have to say that can make a difference? Mankind seems desperate for the answers to these pressing problems.

Why are families divided?

Why are newspapers filled with acts of violence and brutality?

Why is there disturbance in our streets and on our campuses?

Why does our country seem to be going backward instead of forward in human relations?

Why is there war?

Why can't people learn to live together?

What is this sickness that has infested the human race?

How did we get in the middle of the problems that we face today?

To understand the "why" behind the issues we face today, we must go back to the very beginning of the Bible itself. Early in Genesis, chapter 1:27, 28 an emphatic point is made, "And God said, Let us make man in our own image, after our likeness." That is where it all started. Now by the expression, "image of God," we do not mean that man looks like God or that man was a perfect replica of God. Rather, the Bible says that God took man and formed him out of the dust of the earth and then breathed into him the breath of life. And the Bible says that man *became a living soul.*

It was the purpose of an invisible God to create a being who would in a small way reflect His wonderful, magnificent attributes. God then took this perfect creature called man that He made and placed him in a beautiful paradise which the Scripture calls the Garden.

The Lord left this man with some very simple instructions. Of all the trees of the Garden man could freely eat. There was just one exception. The trees represent life and God was saying, in effect, "I want you to live. I want life to be exciting, thrilling and adventurous. I want you to live life to the hilt; I want you to go out under My direction and enjoy life. Of all the trees in the Garden you may freely eat, with this exception." The Bible tells us that there were two kinds of

trees in that Garden. One was called the "tree of life" and
the other was called the "tree of the knowledge of good and
evil." Both represented a particular way of life. The tree of
life represented God Himself.

God was saying, in effect, "If you eat of Me (the word *eat*
means to depend upon), if you *depend upon Me* . . . if you
allow Me to be your life . . . allow Me to be the pivot of your
existence, the ground of your being . . . allow Me to live My
life through you . . . allow Me to do My thing in you, you
will live! Life will be exciting, life will be thrilling, you will
come alive. And all that life can be, you will have, because
I'm alive in you."

So, in essence, all man had to do was decide to live his
life in total dependence upon the God who made him.

But there was another tree in that garden, it was called
the "tree of the knowledge of good and evil," which was the
very antithesis of the "tree of life." It represented selfish independence. In eating of that forbidden tree, one would be
clenching his fist in the face of God, telling God, "Get off my
back. I will be the captain of my own soul, the master of
my own fate. I will do my own thing! I will run my own
life! Nobody (including God) will tell me what to do."

Those were the two options open to man — whether he
would let God live in him, or live for himself. Whether he
would live his life dependent upon the God who made him,
or live his life independent and separated from the God who
made him.

That is the essence of the difference between righteousness
and sin. Righteousness is letting God do His thing in you —
and sin in you is *you,* doing your own thing, apart from
God. Lying, cheating, gambling, murder, greed, immorality,
are just symptoms of that problem. The real issue is whether
you are going to let God do His thing in you or whether you
are going to do your own thing; whether you are going to
live your life in total dependence upon God who made you,

or whether you are going to live your life independent and separated from God altogether while you run your own life. That is the essential difference between righteousness and sin.

The Bible says specifically that the day you decide to do your own thing, the day you decide you are going to eat of that tree — "the tree of the knowledge of good and evil" — the day you decide to become independent from God and run your life, that is the day that "you will surely die."

Some people will say, "That is the problem that hangs me up about you Christians. You're always condemning people to hell, trying to scare people."

Well, God wasn't condemning anyone. He was simply saying, "Look, I'm life. I'm *it;* if you want to live, get plugged into Me. Let Me do My thing in you. But if you don't want to live, do your own thing. I'm giving you a choice. I'm not condemning you; I'm just telling you where it's at."

That is, in essence, what God is saying.

Let me sum it up like this: You go to the nearest appliance store and look at the latest model refrigerator — the very best model with all the optional features. It's the best thing on the market, so you decide to buy it. A couple of days later they ship the refrigerator to you at your home. The men uncrate it, bring it into your house and put it where you want it in the kitchen. There a serviceman tears off the external shielding for you and explains all about how that particular refrigerator works. He shows you the tremendous freezer, the automatic ice-cube maker, water dispenser and all the things that go on inside. The ice cubes can be used as fast as you want them. He shows you where to put all the meat, the vegetables and the dairy products. After he tells you where to put all the food, and describes the various features and concludes his presentation, he picks up the plug on the floor. He says that when you are ready for this thing to operate, all you do is take the plug and push it into that socket in your wall and your refrigerator will begin to function.

And he goes away. You go off to the supermarket and buy a week's supply of food for the refrigerator. You stand back and look at the food crammed into the refrigerator — meat, frozen foods, vegetables, milk, eggs, soft drinks — the whole works. And as you are about to walk away you notice the plug still lying on the floor. You say to yourself, *You know how those servicemen are, they don't always know what they are talking about. He told me I'd have to plug it in, but I spent $500 for this refrigerator and at that price I shouldn't have to bother with a plug.* So you go away.

A couple of days later you come back and discover that everything in the refrigerator that is perishable has perished. Immediately you get angry, start jumping up and down, and say, "Those no-good appliance dealers — I spend hundreds of dollars for this refrigerator, and another hundred dollars to stack the thing with food, and now it's all rotten!"

So you get on the telephone and call the service department. You begin to give them "what-for," laying one word on another until finally, after about half an hour, when you stop for breath, the serviceman asks, "Madam, did you plug it in?"

In other words, don't get angry with him. The refrigerator just can't function without putting the plug in the socket, because the socket is where the life is — and the refrigerator can't work without life.

So God is saying, "I made you in such a way that you don't function until you plug into Me. Now if you choose to live your life without being plugged into Me, then don't blame Me because you perish." That's what God is saying.

In the third chapter of Genesis, the Bible records that Satan, that spiritual being in the universe diametrically opposed to God and His purposes, came to talk to the first man and woman about that tree. And he said something like this, "Hasn't God said that you can eat of every tree in the Garden?" Now God never said that. But one of the tricks of Satan is to take God's Word and twist it to suit his own purposes. All God had said was, "I want you to enjoy life, but do it plugged into Me because that's the only way it will work. You can't do it apart from Me."

There are those who say that if you get plugged into God, you won't enjoy yourself. One of the greatest lies being perpetrated today is that to become a Christian, to be committed to the life God wants of you, is to turn life into a bore — that you will end up being bored to death and that life won't be at all exciting or thrilling. And some Christians have been "conned" on this point and think that they must avoid having a good time. They must give up all pleasure and sit around twiddling their thumbs all day. God is saying that you won't begin to live, life won't be thrilling and adventuresome until you get plugged into Him. And those who seek "the good life" without Him are disillusioned, frustrated and disappointed.

But God had said that the day man decided to become independent of Him, he would surely die. No two ways about it, he would die. The Scripture says that "the soul that sinneth, it shall die." To sin simply means to be independent from God. Don't think about sin as going out and doing bad things — those are only the symptoms. And by stopping people from doing bad things you are not getting rid of sin. You hear a lot of people say we must go out and stop people from taking drugs. That's not the *problem;* it's a symptom. Others say, we have to stop people from drinking. That's not the problem; it's a symptom. Adultery, murder and stealing are not problems. They are only symptoms.

Getting rid of the symptoms doesn't get rid of the disease. That's the same foolish thinking that suggests that by blowing a person's nose you can help him get rid of his cold. His nose is running because he has a cold. If you want to stop his nose from running, then get rid of his cold.

We have to get rid of the disease that causes people to do those things.

Eve says, "We can't touch that tree lest we die." Satan took only one word, a lie, and added it to the truth. He said, "You shall *not* surely die, because God knows that in the day you eat that fruit you will be as gods." Basically, he was saying to her, *"Eve, right now you are a very ignorant woman. Every time I come and ask you about something, you tell me you have to go and find out what the Lord has to say. Has God got you so bottled up . . . are you so dumb . . . are you so ignorant that you can't think for yourself? Do you have to run and find out what the Lord has to say on everything? Can't you stand on your own two feet and think for yourself? Can't you do anything without running to God all the time? Now Eve, if you listen to me, I will liberate you. I will make it possible for you to think for yourself. Be your own God. You see, the reason God doesn't want you to eat of that tree is that the moment you do, your eyes will be opened. You will become as smart as God, and God is afraid of the competition. God is afraid that you will break loose and begin to think for yourself. God wants to keep you bottled up. God doesn't want you to think for yourself. I'll set you free. Besides, it says right in the Scriptures that God created you in His own image, therefore, you have enough 'God' in you to be like God without Him. You don't need God. Think for yourself. Be independent!"*

And the Bible says that the first woman and the first man were caught up in the idea that they could be their own God and run their own lives, and so they took fruit from that tree.

They clenched their fists in the face of God and told Him to leave them alone. In essence, they told God, "We appreciate the fact that You created us and put us into this beautiful world; we're excited about this wonderful world You've put us in, but from here on out, we'll do things on our own. We'll do it ourselves."

Now what happened?

Three things happened. The first thing was that man decided to become his own God. He *sinned* by telling God to "get off his back" and leave him alone. Keep in mind at this point what sin is — rebellion against God.

Stop getting hung up on the peripheral issues.

You may be the most moral person in the world.

You may go to church every Sunday.

You may have been baptized.

You may sing in the choir in your church.

You may be a deacon or an usher.

You may believe in God's person.

You may read the Bible every day.

You may be the epitome of what a good moral person ought to be.

But if you are doing your own thing, making your own plans and running your own life *independent* of God, that makes you as much a sinner as the prostitute or thief, because these sins are symptomatic of the basic sin — life apart from God.

So, the first thing that sin did was separate man from God. Man lost one of the most priceless possessions he could ever have — the ability to relate to God. He lost his personal knowledge of God. Man no longer understood what it meant for him to be in God and for God to be in him. When a man detaches himself from God, it's like not having the plug in the socket. He no longer functions as he was created to function. Because, you see, *you need God to even be a man. You can't be a complete man, or a complete woman without the life of God.* And the problem in our world today is that large numbers of people do not know God. Ask them. Stop the average man on the street.

"Do you know God?"

"Well, I go to church every Sunday."

"No, I didn't ask you that. Do you know God?"

"Well, I sing in the choir."

"No, no, no; you missed my point. Do you know God?"

"Well, I'm a deacon."

"No. Do you know God?"

"Well, I've been baptized. I've been confirmed. I've been to confession."

"No, no! Do you know God?

"Well, I can quote some Bible verses."

"But do you know God?"

Being religious doesn't mean you know God. Everyone is basically religious. Everyone belongs to something. You can join some churches easier and faster than you can join fraternal organizations. I know you can probably join the church. I'm not talking about that. I'm asking, "Do you know God?"

We have produced a sterile form of religion. That is the sad situation that we face in our country today. People can be religious without having a personal knowledge of God. In fact, most people — even very religious people — are living their lives detached from God. That is the problem of our world today.

Because men don't know God, the world is messed up.

Because men don't know God, *people* are messed up.

Because men don't know God, families are divided.

Because men don't know God, we have wars.

Because men don't know God, we have hunger and poverty.

Because men don't know God, we have racism and bigotry.

We have hate — *because men don't know God.*

Sin has certainly separated man from God.

The second thing about sin is that it separated man from his brother. Not too long after the first man sinned, his son, Cain, rose up and killed his brother, Abel. When a man loses fellowship with God he has no sense of responsibility to his brother. That is precisely why the world is in a mess. People just can't get along together without God. The number one issue we face in American society today is whether we can go on living together.

According to the Kerner report, the white and black communities are two societies, separate and unequal. Maybe that's why, when I was a kid, I had difficulty singing songs like *Onward Christian Soldiers* — "we are not divided, all one body we." People were fighting all the time, there was no way they could talk about being one.

These same people also wanted me to get up and affirm, "I pledge allegiance to the flag of the United States of America, to the Republic for which it stands, *one nation. . . .*" Well, I said, that's not true, we're *not* one nation. All you have to do is ask one of the 500,000 American Indians in this country if we are one nation. Talk to the 22 million black Americans; talk to a few thousand Mexican-Americans, to Puerto Ricans — or any of the other minority groups that are being stepped on because of institutionalized racism in America. Then you will understand that we are not "one."

We are *not* one because men are not plugged into God. Consequently, there is no way we can get plugged into each other. It's not only a problem of man against man, race against race, religion against religion, culture against culture, but even within the *same race* and within the *same culture,* there are problems. As an example, where I live (and you know where I live), I have *three locks* on my door — and it's not "Charlie" I'm trying to keep out.

So, you see, you have people divided regardless of their race, regardless of their skin color. You have people who are against each other . . . period! — whites against whites, blacks against blacks, Indians against Indians, and so on. And if that doesn't cause enough problems, you pit Indian against white, white against black, black against Puerto

Rican, and pretty soon the whole human race is completely fouled up. *And until we recognize that, we're in trouble.*

There is something profoundly wrong with the human race. Men are separated from each other because they are separated from God and can't solve either side of their problem.

Finally, sin even separated man from himself. Man no longer understood why he was here, what life was all about. He became confused and frustrated. He lost his sense of identity. If you look at the world today you discover that we are facing a unique identity crisis. People are trying to find out who they are. They're trying to put their thing together. If you listen closely to the pop songs of our generation, you will notice many of them are speaking out of the same despair and frustration. "Who can bring us together, who can help me discover myself?" Listen to words — whether by Simon and Garfunkel, Lou Rawls, The Fifth Dimension, the Mamas and the Papas or the Rolling Stones — they are all saying the same thing.

"Who can help me out of my dilemma?"

"What's the name of the game?"

"What's it all about, Alfie?"

"Who's going to help me put my thing together?"

They're all asking *How am I going to get myself together? — who's going to help me figure out who I am?*

A few offer some solutions. They say that man can solve his problem through education. Will it work? If we could educate people and get them more informed, would that bring people together? Will that plug them into God? Will that get rid of the immorality in our nation? At this moment we happen to live in the most informed period of history. Information in our country *doubles* every six years, we are told. Last semester's textbook is obsolete this semester because of the fantastic increase in knowledge. The average high school student who graduates today knows more about the physical laws of our universe than some of the greatest scientists of just twenty years ago. Our young people today already know more about what's happening. You can speak to any fifteen-year-old today and discover that he knows more than his parents discovered by the age of thirty. We *are* an informed people. We have all kinds of knowledge and wisdom at our disposal. We *are* an educated society. Yet, with all of our education and all of our information, we haven't been able to bring ourselves together. Still we haven't been able to eliminate the problems of the human race.

So education is obviously *not* the answer.

"Experts" also told us we could solve our problems through economics. If we could just produce a more affluent society, they suggested, life would be a Utopia. Surely, they said, if we could give people more of this world's goods, enough to eat, enough money, enough shelter, supply them with the material goods of life, that would solve our problem. They looked at some of the neighborhoods that were exploding and said the reason why a kid throws a brick through a window is that he doesn't have enough. *"If we could supply him with enough we could change his whole outlook,"* they reason.

But if that's true, how do you explain going two miles south of that poor neighborhood to the university campus? Here is an upper-middle class kid whose old man *owns* the system and he is throwing bricks, too!

He ransacks the school files, he burns the administration building, cuts the telephone lines, and battles with police. That kid is arrested and he has *Carte Blanche, Diner's Club* and *American Express* cards in his pocket. He has charge cards to the major department stores in town. When the average poor kid was trying to get his first bicycle, he was driving his first T-Bird! Yet, he, too, is saying, "Let's burn the system!" He has money, he's being educated, his family owns the system. He can have anything he wants.

Can you imagine these two passing each other on the street?

The poor kid is saying to the rich kid, "I'm on my way to the system. You 'cats' done locked me out for 400 years and I'm on my way to the system to get a piece of the action."

"Let me tell you something," says the rich kid. "I just *left* the system. My old man owns it and I'm burning it!"

In other words, economics is not the answer.

Now, I'm not saying the poor kid shouldn't fight for justice for poor people. I'm saying that if all we're going to fight for is simply to feed the hungry, we're not going far enough. We must not only put bread in a man's belly and a roof over his head, get him a job with identity and dignity, but we must also get him plugged in to where life is really at — life with God.

The affluent society has already proven to us that economic security and affluence is not enough. The world is being messed up by wealthy people who don't know how to run the world. Economics is not enough.

The third "answer" these experts gave us was religion. "Religion will bring us together," they reasoned. "Get people religious and that will solve the problem." So we came up with religion as an answer to mankind's pressing problems. Some even instituted a very Americanized kind of religious atmosphere. We all became "religious." But you see, you can be "religious" without having anything to do with God. That's the problem in our country, most people are religious — but they don't know God. You can stop the average American on the street and he can quote at least one Bible verse. Most Americans believe that there is a God somewhere. Forty percent of the American people to to church every Sunday. We're "religious," all right.

Yet, with all the religion, churches and creeds, why haven't we been able to come together? Why haven't we been able to plug people back in to God? Civilization is a chronicle of man trying to find a way back to God, back to his brother, back to himself.

And the search has been futile. The Scriptures tell us that the heavens and the earth were searched for someone to bring men and God together. It was Job (I've given him a modern man's vocabulary) who cried out, "Is there someone in the universe who can understand me as a man; someone who understands what it means to be weak, and limited and tempted; what it means to be sinful flesh like I am? Who understands what it means to have limitations of a man? I need someone who does understand all my limitations, all of my sin, all of my degradation — someone who can grab me by one hand and reach out and grab hold of the Holy God with the other hand and bring us together." And the Bible says, "In the fulness of time (the appointed economy of God), God decided to do something about the situation." God decided to become a man. You see there was no man in the universe who could bring men back to God because the whole human race was infested with sin. Every person born into the world was born independent from God. Every man born was born with this cancerous disease of sin in him. There was no one in the human race who could bring men back to God, so God solved the problem by coming to man. The apostle John puts it this way, "In the beginning was the Word, and the Word was with God, and the Word was God" (John 1:1). Now if it had stopped there, my reply would have been "So what?" But about a dozen verses later it says, "And the Word became flesh." God put on the garb of humanity and walked the earth as a man. For the first time in the history of the human race since Adam another man has come to earth to bring men back to God.

There were only two men in all of history who walked the face of the earth who had the ability to be what God wanted them to be. The first one was Adam, the first man, who said, "I don't want to be what God wants." He sinned, and genetically the whole human race became infected with sin. And the "last Adam," Jesus Christ, came to earth to try to undo what the first Adam had done. We have to watch Him very closely. We have to check Jesus out. We have to make sure that He isn't like any other man. Because if He acts like any other man, then He, too, is in trouble. As He walks the earth for the 33½ years that He lives, we have to watch Him to make sure He doesn't do anything wrong. We have to watch Him to make sure that He never acts independent of His Heavenly Father. And sure enough, if you keep your eyes on Christ, you discover He never did wrong. In fact, Jesus never did anything. He never healed the sick, raised the dead, gave sight to the blind, or performed miracles. He never did a thing. You say, "Now wait a minute, Tom, hold it! That's heresy! Everyone knows that Jesus Christ did all these things."

No, absolutely not. Jesus Christ was the only man who ever walked the face of the earth who never did anything. His Heavenly Father did it all. Listen to what He says in effect in John chapter 5, beginning with verse 30, "That which I do my Father does in me. I do only those things which please my Father. I have not come to do my will but the will of my Father who sent me." In essence He said to His own disciples, "I don't want you to believe Me just because you see Me heal the sick, raise the dead, or bring sight to the blind; I don't want you to believe Me just because I'm performing miracles. But I want you to believe Me that the miracles I perform are because of My Father working in and through Me. If you ever see Me doing something that My Father is not doing in Me, then you don't have to believe in Me. But if I'm doing what My Father tells Me to do, then you had better give attention to Me."

For the years Jesus walked the face of the earth, He did only those things which His Father told Him to do and He did only those things which His Father did in and through

Him. He lived His life in total dependency upon His Father. That was the difference between the first Adam and the last Adam.

The first Adam said, "I will do it myself."

The last Adam says, "I've come to do the will of My Father." There's the difference.

You will understand something of Jesus' character when you see how He was tempted in the wilderness. Jesus had fasted forty days. He hadn't eaten and was hungry. Satan came to Him and said, "If You are the Son of God why don't You command that these stones be turned into bread?"

Now what in the world is sinful about making bread out of stones? Nothing. Then why would the devil ask Him to do a ridiculous thing like make bread out of stones? Very simple. Satan was simply saying, "Jesus Christ, You are the Son of God; You are God's Son. You Yourself said You come from God. If You *are* the Son of God, then You have enough God in You to be like God without God. So why don't You turn those stones into bread by Yourself? You don't have to check it out with Your Father." Satan knew if he could get Jesus to do one thing independent of His Father, then Jesus, too, would have sinned. But the exciting thing about Christ was that He never once made a move without His Father. That's why He was perfect. And the Bible says that because He was perfect, He was worthy to substitute for us in meeting God's demands for our sins.

One night, while mapping out strategy for a gang fight, I heard from a radio speaker that Jesus Christ, God's Son came to earth for the purpose of assuming the sinful nature with which I was born. I had a problem about Jesus Christ. Although most of what I learned about Jesus Christ, I learned within a church setting, He never came across as relevant to my problems. You see, where I lived in a neighborhood of 4,000 people living within one block, fifty-seven percent of them grew up without their fathers. There were drug addicts,

pimps and all kinds of other unsavory types. I said if I'm going to trust the Saviour, I'll need a Christ who can survive
all of this, so He'd better be tough. But in the pictures that
they offered me of Jesus, He didn't look tough. All the pictures they ever drew of Christ made Him look like a white,
middle-class softy. He looked very effeminate, with nice soft
hands — as if they'd just been washed in Dove. And I said
to myself, there is *no way* I can commit myself to that kind
of Jesus. He didn't seem tough enough to survive in my
neighborhood. I said we could do Him in on any street corner and we wouldn't even have to wait until dark. He just
didn't have what it took.

But I learned something new that night as I listened to the
radio. I learned that the Christ who leaped out of the pages
of the New Testament was nobody's softy. I learned that
Jesus Christ was a "gutsy," radical, contemporary revolutionary with hair on His chest and dirt under His fingernails. He
was the kind of Jesus Christ who knew where the action was.
In fact, the Bible says He went out and rubbed shoulders with
the kinds of people whom I knew in my neighborhood.

I also discovered that Jesus could tell the Establishment off
when they needed it. What He did took guts — to stand up
in front of the Establishment of His day and say: "You generation of vipers, you hypocrites, you graveyards, you're like
dead men's bones." Does that sound soft to you? Jesus
walked into the temple where they had desecrated the house
of His Father and He overturned the money tables and drove
out the money changers. He was a tough Jesus.

But, beyond being tough, Jesus was also compassionate.
He was the Jesus who could look at a prostitute and tell her
that her sins were forgiven. He was the Christ who could
stand up and weep over a city. He was the Christ who
rubbed shoulders with people of ill repute, who opened His
arms to them, and made Himself available to them. That
kind of Christ.

I had another problem that kept me from Jesus Christ. As I mentioned earlier, anyone can prove society is messed up. I said to myself, the church is in the society, and the church seems to reflect the values of the society as a whole — the bad values as well as the good. I reasoned that if the society is corrupt, then the church must be corrupt as well. When they told me that Jesus Christ was the head of the church, I said there must be something wrong with Him too. I had a problem until I discovered, in the New Testament, the nature of the real church. I learned the real church wasn't an institutionalized form of society's corruption — like many of the churches I'd seen. It wasn't like a lot of the foolishness, hypocrisy, and people playing games with God which I had seen. I read the Bible and I saw for the first time that Jesus Christ came to call people not necessarily to a church or to an institution, but He came to call people to Himself.

They took this Christ and nailed Him to a cross. They didn't nail Him to a cross just because He was a religious leader who was too radical for His time. No, on that cross Jesus Christ was bearing my sinful nature. I learned that God had literally taken Tom Skinner and put him up on that cross with Christ; and that when Christ was crucified, Tom Skinner's old nature was crucified.

I was told that Jesus shed His blood to forgive me of all my sin — sin that was a result of my independence . . . of my acting apart from God. Three days later, I was told, Jesus Christ arose from the dead. He didn't get up out of the grave just to prove that He had power over death. No, He arose so that any person who dared commit his life to Him, could have Christ's resurrected life in him.

When I heard all that, as I said, I was mapping out strategy for one of the largest street wars ever to take place in New York City. Over the radio I heard that Christ came to die in my place, to take on my punishment and provide me with forgiveness. I learned that Christ rose from the dead to live in me — that He was prepared to send me out into a real world, making me a radically new person. He was prepared to turn me on to what God intended a man to be.

I responded to that Christ!

I found myself bowing my head next to that radio that night and praying a very simple prayer: "Lord, I don't understand all of this, I don't dig You, I don't know what You're at, but I do know that I need You. And based on that, I now give You the right to take over my life. If these things are true, I give You the right to come inside and live in me."

Do you know what happened that night? I had no traumatic experience, I saw no blinding flashes of light, heard no thunder roar. No mountains caved in. I felt no tingling up my spine, but Jesus Christ, the Son of God, took up residence in my life, and He has been living there ever since. My life has never been the same. And the most exciting part about it is from that moment on I have not made any effort to become a Christian. There are large numbers of people who think that to be a Christian, you carry around in your inside pocket a list of rules and regulations. You keep them close by. And the rules say; one — don't do this; two — stay away from this; three — don't touch that; four — don't go near that, don't look at that and stay away from *that!* The list is endless. And some would have you go out and hold yourself real tight, trying real hard to be a Christian, looking real sanctimonious. Some of the most neurotic people I know are religious people trying to be Christians. Because you see, my friend, *you can't be a Christian; it's impossible.* If you could *be* a Christian, there would be no need for Jesus Christ. But Christianity means Christ living His own life in and through you without assistance from you. Because Jesus Christ doesn't need your help to be Jesus Christ.

There are many people trying to "help" God. God doesn't need our help. He made heaven and earth without us. God

became a man without us. In Christ He died and rose again
without us. He ascended back to heaven without our assistance. Why should we think He now needs our help to run
a life? He doesn't — all He needs from you in your *availability*.

As you commit yourself to Him, Christ will come inside
and live His life through you. The Christian life is not something you try to do. You can't do it. You can't be like
Christ any more than you can be like any other person. If
I gave you eight hours of practice for the next ten years to be
exactly like some other person, could you do it? No, because
you're two distinct human beings. No human being can be
like another one. So how in all the world — if you can't be
like another human being — can you be like Jesus? You
can't. The exciting "good news" is that Jesus Christ will be
Himself in you. That's what it is all about. Instead of you
going out breaking your neck trying to be a Christian, all
Christ says is, "Look, why don't you just invite Me to live in
you? I will come inside and be a Christian in you. I will
live My own life through you. I will be your righteousness. I
will be your holiness. I will produce the love, peace, and
patience in you. All you have to do is just be available."

Would you like that to happen to you right now? As a
result of inviting Christ into my life I know who I am now.
I know who I am — I'm God's son. I'm a member of the
royal family of God which puts me in the best family stock
there is in all the world. *I know who I am.*

I've also discovered that you can't label or pigeonhole Jesus
Christ. He's not an American, any more than He's a Russian;
not a Democrat any more than a Republican; not a capitalist
any more than He's a communist. He is the Lord of heaven
and earth and He expects me to respond to Him as Lord.

The other beautiful thing I've discovered is that to be a
Christian, I don't have to give up my blackness. I was worried about that. I've discovered that Jesus Christ lives His

life through my redeemed blackness. I haven't had to give up my blackness to become a Christian any more than Jesus Christ wants you to give up your culture. All He asks is that you give up yourself. And as you make yourself available to Him, He will live His life through you. It's exciting.

Also, I now know what my responsibility to people is. All I ask is that people give me the opportunity to love them. Whether they love me back is not important. I derive enough love through my relationship with Jesus Christ to be able to survive without their love. But I do ask that they give me the privilege to love them. That doesn't mean I let people walk all over me. When a person walks all over me, he is not only dehumanizing me but he is dehumanizing himself — and I love him too much to let him dehumanize himself. So I won't let him walk all over me. But I do ask that he give me the privilege of loving him. And Jesus Christ has provided me the power to do it — His resurrected life is now living in me. I stand as a completely new person. Jesus Christ has completely transformed my life. I submit to you that if He could do it for me, He can certainly do it for you.

The question is *do you want Him to?*

2

The Greatest Revolutionary Ever

I'm convinced that when historians come to document our time, they are going to be forced to call this an age of revolution. It comes as no real surprise to us. We have seen more changes, more revolutions, than any other generation in the history of men.

Even today, as we look around, we see the drama of revolution unfolding in nearly every area of life. Remembering that the word "revolution" means "change" helps us see this even more clearly, for we see economic changes, social changes, political changes, as well as changes in fashions, life-styles and attitudes of people.

But what about it? Granted, it is a time of revolution — of change. Are these changes bringing any hope to those who despair of finding solutions to mankind's most pressing problems? Will these revolutionary ideas, changes or developments ever come up with a society that is the way it ought to be? Only time will tell.

It is interesting to look back at recent revolutionary changes — let's say those which have occurred within the past one hundred years. Did you know that most of these revolutions were accomplished by a small group of people? Never the majority. Most good changes, most relevant changes, have not been brought about by a great number of people, but by a small group of people who looked at an existing situation and decided the system needed to be changed. And, against overwhelming odds, they went out to change it.

Someone has said, "Ten percent of the people are actively engaged in progressive change; ten percent of the people are actively engaged in resisting change and the other eighty percent just sit there." Someone else has said, "There are the few people who make things happen; the many people who watch things happen; and the overwhelming majority of people who have no idea what is happening." And that is the problem of our society. In the age and generation in which we live, the overwhelming majority of the people in America today have absolutely no idea what is happening.

Right or wrong, most of the changes in the world are being brought about by a handful of people who are basically saying there needs to be revolution.

As you review history, you will also discover that most changes are brought about by young people. More than half the people alive in our country right now were born since 1945 — which clearly puts young people in the majority. And many of these young people are saying, "The system has to be changed . . . the world has to be changed." These young people are committed to not leaving the world the way they found it. It's an age of revolution.

In fact, in 1848 a young German sat down in a small room in Germany and decided the world needed political and economic change. He put his thoughts on paper and later printed his philosophy in pamphlets which he entitled *Das Kapital*. He spread these booklets throughout Europe. Some people read the pamphlets, but most people ignored them. Just a few people around the world thought his ideas had some value. Sixty years later, in a small run-down room, a young Russian sat down and read those writings and decided they could work. He went throughout Russia trying to sell people on these new political and economic ideas. Again, only a handful of people believed in them.

One day this young Russian stood up in the middle of a town square and spoke to a large group of people about the need to bring about revolutionary change in his country. At the end of his fiery, passionate speech he said to all standing there, "Those of you who are ready to die for the cause of the revolution in Russia . . . those of you who are prepared to give your lives that a revolution might take place, I call you to step out of the crowd and join the revolution." What was the response? The fantastic number of seventeen people stepped forward. Not enough to shake up the inside of a garbage can. But those seventeen people went out and convinced others of their cause. Before long, they became seventeen thousand people; and then forty thousand people. By 1921 Lenin had complete control of Russia and today Communism controls more than two-fifths of the world's population. Why? Because one man had an idea and the guts to stick by it — and he created a revolution.

In the early part of this century men began to manufacture a funny looking thing they called an automobile. To make it run, you got out in front of it and cranked a motor, then jumped in quickly, pressed down on a pedal and the thing started moving. There were people who began to fight this new contraption that sputtered down the streets, scaring horses and people. People made wise cracks about the sanity of people who drove this funny thing called an automobile. They laughed and said, "Get a horse!"

Then it became serious as doctors began to issue reports. They said, "The automobile speeding at ten miles an hour is more than the human heart can stand. We demand that all automobiles be removed from the road!"

When the automobile speed increased to the fantastic rate of thirty miles an hour, scientists and biologists said, "The human body will never be able to take it. Get it off the road!"

But the people who invented and developed the automobile stuck by their guns and today we speed along modern highways at seventy miles an hour (and if there is no fuzz some take it at ninety!). And our bodies still stand it. Simply because someone had an idea, and the guts to stick by it in the face of opposition. We have revolutionized our whole way of living through the automobile. There is no other machine in society that has so revolutionized the travel life, sex life, work habits and the whole life style of America as has the automobile. Because someone had the guts to stick by an idea and create a revolution.

About the same time two brothers were fooling around in their backyard with a funny looking machine. They said it was actually going to take off from the ground and fly. And then the word began to spread that these young guys were building this "flying machine"; people said, "Those young whippersnappers are fooling around with things they don't understand. If God intended man to fly He would have given him wings." Even in churches people got up and denounced these young men who challenged God's air space. Well, they got that crate off the ground and it wobbled a few feet in the air — perhaps the distance of a football field. Today we jet around the world at 700 miles an hour. By 1973 manufacturers will be building supersonic jets that will travel at 1,800 m.p.h. so you will be able to fly from Chicago to Los Angeles in one hour and forty-five minutes. Why? Because someone had an idea, the guts to stick by it, and he created a revolution.

In the early 1930's, Germany had just come out of World War I. Germany had been defeated and was the laughing stock of the world. Her military and political systems were in chaos. There were riots, disobedience, conflict and lawlessness in the streets. And a young German arose and said to his people, "If I am elected I will restore Germany to a place of prominence." Germany had a war debt that amounted to several billion dollars. He said, "If I am elected I will settle the billions of dollars that we owe the rest of the world. We just won't pay it." He promised, "I will build a military force that will be undefeated by the nations of the world. I will produce a young people's army that will be revered by the nations of the world. I will produce a super-race of men in Germany who will be untouched by the races of men." In 1932 he was elected. By 1936 he had complete control of his country. By 1941 Adolph Hitler had plunged the entire world into war. Why? Because one man had an idea, the guts to stick by it — and he created a revolution.

It was 1959. A young Latin-American, with some country-men, took a look at his nation and decided it needed to be changed. So he and a few of his fellows went from one village and hamlet to another, convincing other young men and women that they needed to join the revolution. Through guerilla warfare they attacked and conquered villages and hamlets. Along the way they picked up idealistic young people who left their homes, jobs, parents and schools to join the revolution.

One day these young people announced that they were going to march on the capital of their nation and take over the whole country. Word of what these young people planned reached Moscow, Paris, London and Washington — but no one really took them serious. So-called world experts said, "They don't understand international diplomacy; they're not schooled in the economic and political philosophies of the world; they do not understand the ins and outs of political process. They will never make it."

But Fidel Castro and his followers marched into Havanna and they've been sitting there ever since. Because one guy had an idea, the guts to stick by it, and he created a revolution.

On December 18, 1960, four black guys sat down in a lounge in A & T College in Greensboro, North Carolina, to "chew the fat" as they did most afternoons. One of the fellows said, "You know, I think I'm going into town to eat my dinner instead of eating in the school cafeteria."

One of the other fellows said, "Where do you plan to eat?"

The first said, "Well, they've just built this new restaurant down on Main Street and I'm going down there to check out the food."

One of the other guys grinned sarcastically, "What you mean is you're going in the back door and have them serve you through the back window, and bring the food back here because you know they don't serve colored people down there."

"Well," he said, "I'm not going to ask for them to serve me any colored people. I'm going to ask for some fried chicken and I'm going to sit there till they serve me."

And those four boys went down and sat at that lunch counter and started a wave of social demonstrations across America that turned America upside down. Why? Because one man had an idea, the guts to stick by it, and he created a revolution.

I am not here to discuss the rightness or wrongness of these revolutions I have listed.

I am here merely to remind you that we live in an hour of revolutionary change. And there is no doubt about it — revolution is coming one way or the other. We live in an age of change and anyone who wants to survive in the world today, who wants to be relevant to the issues today, has to be revolutionary.

What is a revolution? The word, as we mentioned, simply means "change." But in our contemporary usage, revolution is to take an existing situation which has proved to be unworkable, old-fashioned, archaic, impractical, out-of-date and tear it down to replace it with a system that works. That's revolution. Most of the so-called revolutionaries running around the streets are saying, "That's what we need to do." Whether we agree with them or not is incidental. The issue is that a revolution is bent on changing things.

Now if you go back through history you will discover that there have been some great revolutionaries. People like Plato and Socrates were revolutionaries in the philosophical world. There were military and political revolutionaries like Karl Marx, Lenin, Hitler, Julius Caesar, Mussolini. If you look in the social realm, there have been revolutionaries — Gandhi, Martin Luther King, Malcolm X, or Bobby Seale.

The world has seen an army of men who have gone out and tried to change the system. There have been great and terrible figures who have appeared through history to change this world.

Of all the historical research I have done . . . of all the revolutions I have read about . . . of all the revolutionary leaders I have studied — I am convinced that the greatest revolutionary of all time is Jesus Christ. Of all the men who walked the face of the earth to bring about true radical change, Jesus Christ, God's Son, the man from heaven, was the greatest revolutionary who ever lived.

You say, "Now wait a minute. You mean that Jesus Christ was a revolutionary?" That's right. Remember our definition — revolution is to take an existing situation which has proved to be unworkable, archaic, impractical, and tear it down or replace it with a system that works. In line with this, check Second Corinthians 5:17 — "Therefore, if any man be in Christ, he is a new creature; old things have passed away; behold, all things are become new." Notice the revolutionary content of that verse. "If any man be in Christ he is a new creature." The purpose of a revolution is to bring about a new order. "Old things have passed away." The aim of a revolution is to do away with that which is old. "All things are become new." The thrust of a revolution is to replace the old system with one that works. That is what makes Jesus

Christ more radical than any of the so-called revolutionaries today.

I sometimes talk with people who claim to be radicals. They say, "Man, we're going to get rid of the system. The system has got to go."

When you ask them, "What are you going to replace the system with?" They say, "That's irrelevant. The important thing is that we get rid of the system."

Well, if you're going to ask me to shed my blood for a revolutionary program, you'd better give me the whole program. Don't tell me that what you're going to replace the system with is incidental! If you're going to ask me to break my neck to bring about change, tell me what you have to replace the present set-up. Jesus Christ came not only to change the system, but to replace it with something that would work. That's the aim of a revolution.

What was it that made Jesus Christ so radical? Keeping in mind that the word "radical" means "root" — a radical is a person who gets to the "root" of a problem, a person who gets down to the foundations of what is wrong. What made Jesus Christ so radical? I believe what made Jesus Christ radical was the fact that He was the only man who walked the face of the earth, who lived His life in total dependency upon the Father who sent Him. All other people who ever lived came to do their own thing. They came to run their own lives. All other men who ever lived basically came to do what was best for them. So when you hear people say, "I'm going out to do my own thing," what they really mean is, "I plan to run my own life." And the sin of the world is the fact that most people are doing their own thing, running their own lives, becoming their own gods. Jesus Christ was the only man who ever walked the face of the earth who never had His own way; never did what He wanted; never did anything to please Himself. In effect, Jesus Christ said, "That which I do, My Father does it in me. I come to do only those things which will please the Father. I've come to do the will of My Father who has sent Me."

Time and time again you will notice that every move Jesus Christ made, He made in complete dependency upon the Father who sent Him. Every word Christ spoke, His Father from heaven spoke through Him. Every deed He performed, His Father from heaven did in Him. Every action He undertook was the action of His Father. Christ was the only man who made Himself totally available to the Father from heaven, and walked the earth the way God wanted man to walk the earth. That is why Jesus Christ was radical. When He came to earth, He came to start a revolution. And every revolution has to have people who will join it, people who will follow the revolutionary leader.

Some time ago, I read a pamphlet written by an unknown author. He was a revolutionary. He did not believe in God, or the Scriptures, and he wanted nothing to do with Jesus Christ. He was a revolutionist in the sense that he wanted to bring about violent change. And in his book he said there are three basic ingredients that every revolutionist must have if he wants to change the world. I would like to share those ingredients with you. And I would like to ask you, based on those ingredients, can you qualify as a true revolutionist? Remember, there is no way you can survive in the world; no way you can make a significant contribution to the world; no way you can help change a messed-up system — unless you're willing to become radical.

Now here's what happens. This revolutionary said the first thing you must do to be a true revolutionary is give up yourself for the cause of the revolution. Listen to the words of Jesus Christ, the greatest revolutionary who ever lived. In Matthew 16:24 Jesus said in effect, "If any man will come after Me, if any man would be My disciple, if any man would by My revolutionary, let him deny himself, take up his cross, and follow Me." Let him *deny himself*. The word "deny" means to "ignore," to disregard. It means to have nothing to do with. Basically what Jesus is saying is this: "You want to be My revolutionary? Then I demand that you ignore yourself, that you have nothing to do with yourself. If you want to follow Me you must disregard yourself in order to be My disciple."

Now why would Jesus ask you to give up yourself? Why would He ask you to ignore yourself? Is it because Jesus Christ was some kind of an egotistical maniac, so caught up with Himself that He wanted everyone else to be nothing? Why does Jesus make such a demand? If you want to be His revolutionist, if you are going out to change the system in His name, become a part of a new order to bring about change — why does He ask you to give up yourself? Jesus Christ knew that at the bottom of all the problems of humanity is man himself. The biggest problem we face in the world today is *people*.

Ourselves.

Many of the so-called radicals today make a sad mistake in thinking the system happens to be "things." You hear people say, "Man, we gotta get the system. Let's get General Motors." And so they march down to a General Motors building, throw fire bombs in the building, burn the building down. They walk away and say, "Man, we got General Motors." They haven't *touched* General Motors. Because what happens? The next day, the men on the Board of Directors of General Motors call a meeting, find a new location, buy new land and build a new building. *That's* General Motors . . . the men . . . not the building. It's people. If you want to change General Motors, you've got to change the people.

Now what Jesus is saying is that people are messed up. And because people are messed up, the system is messed up.

People say, "America is a racist society." I agree. But

America is a racist society because people are racists.

People say, "America is an immoral society." That's true. But America is an immoral society because people in it are immoral.

So ultimately, if you want to change society you must change people.

Jesus was saying people are messed up. In essence He is saying that there is no room in the kingdom of God for messed up people. Therefore, if you want to be My revolutionary, Jesus is saying, you must deny yourself . . . disregard and ignore yourself.

The Kingdom of God is only for "together" people. But you can't come together until you're willing to recognize that you need to "give up" yourself. That *you* are the problem; that humanity is the problem; and the human race is made up of people. Most of America's problems revolve around people. This is what a vast number of young people in America today are saying — that *people* in the system are messed up, and somehow we have to *change* people.

Perhaps for the first time in our generation, there are young people in America who are dedicated to moral change. Now I'm not saying that these young people are any more moral than their parents, or any more moral than the generation before them. But they are challenging the American system, saying that America is immoral and you can't cover up that immorality with a Brooks Brothers suit, matching tie, clean-shaven face and short hair.

These people are saying the system needs to be changed and you can only change it by changing people. And that's what Christ is saying. Jesus says, "If you want to change the system, you have to change people. And you can only change people when you begin with yourself. If you want to follow Me, deny yourself. The man who follows Me must deny himself."

In the seventh chapter of Romans, the apostle Paul gives

a classic example of the whole problem of the human race
— the inability of people to do what they want to do. In
essence he says, "In my mind I want to serve God. In my
mind I want to do the will of God. In my mind I want to do
what is right. But," he says, "I can't do what is right."

Paul tells us, "Every time I would do good, evil is present
with me. Every time I try to lift myself above the common
level to be what God wants me to be, there is something that
drags me back down." And he cries out, "Oh, wretched man
that I am! Who shall deliver me from the body of this
death?"

Historians tell us that during Paul's day, when a man committed a murder and they caught up with him, they chained
him back to back to the lifeless, stinking corpse of the man
he had killed. The murderer was sentenced to carry the
corpse of the man he murdered. The apostle Paul is saying,
"There's a corpse on me. Every time I would be what God
wants, there is something that drags me down. Every time
I would do good, evil is present with me. Every time I would
speak the truth I end up lying. Every time I try to walk
right, I turn the wrong way. Every time I try to love, I end
up being hateful. Every time I try to be patient, I end up
being irritable. I just don't seem capable of being what I
want. Who shall deliver me?"

What he is saying is, "I'm messed up and I need help."
And that's the problem. We are messed up. Even if you go
back to the inception of our country you will find that men
were powerless to live up to what they wanted to be. They
made plenty of noble speeches about liberty, justice, freedom and tranquillity. Many of these people, I am sure, believed what they were saying. I believe most of them were
sincere. But I don't believe that they had the *power* to follow
through with what they said. For example, with the British
breathing down the early Colonists' backs, Patrick Henry stood
up in the House of Congress and said, "I don't know what

course others may take, but as for me, give me liberty or give me death." Now I believe he meant that. I mean, I firmly believe that when Patrick Henry said, "Give me liberty or give me death," he meant it. But he would have had his mind blown if two or three of *his slaves* would have said, "Me, too!" You see, Patrick Henry did not have the power to let his own slaves go, even though he believed in liberty and freedom. What we believe theoretically and what we are able to execute pragmatically are two different things.

Most people in the human race know right from wrong. Most of us know what we ought to do. But our question is, where do we get the power to do what we ought to do? What Jesus is saying is this: "You don't have the power to do what you want to do. Man in himself is incapable of carrying out his noble ambitions and his noble ideas. Man is a sinner. Man is by nature born in sin. Man is born alienated from God. Man is independent from God. And by virtue of being independent from God, man doesn't have the power to be what God wants." Jesus is also saying, "Until you recognize you are powerless; until you recognize you don't have what it takes to be what God wants and are prepared to 'give up' yourself, there is no hope for changing the human race."

You must give up yourself.

"If any man therefore deny himself, take up his cross. . . ." *Take up his cross.* A lot of people, when they hear the word "cross," think of suffering. Right away they think that because they are suffering it must mean that they are already Christians. Job said, "Man is born unto trouble as the sparks fly upward." In other words, all you have to do to have trouble in your life is *just be born.* Once you're born into the human race, you've had it. So simply because you've had a tough time, doesn't mean God is automatically on your side. It is very easy for those of us who are victims of racism or oppression to assume God is on our side. We figure this way; God is a God of love and on the side of the underdog. I'm the underdog. Therefore, God must be on my side. But that's bad reasoning. God is not on *anyone's* side. The point is are *you* hanging with God? The question is whether you're committing yourself to *Him*.

What Jesus is really saying is this: "If any man would be My revolutionary, let him give up himself, take up his cross and *die.*" Not suffer — but die! "Now wait a minute," you say. "You mean I'm supposed to roll over in the grave and die?"

No. The word death here means "to be unresponsive." When I was in high school and college I did a lot of acting. I remember that if you didn't go out on the stage in the first or second scene, you always asked those who were in the first or second scene (the minute they came backstage), "What kind of audience do we have tonight? Are they dead or alive?" In other words — did they laugh at the jokes, applaud the scenes and respond to what was happening on stage? If they did, we would say the audience was alive. But if the actors went out and got no laughs at the jokes and little response, then the audience was dead. The point was whether the audience was *responding*. To be dead, therefore, means to be unresponsive. A dead person *can't* respond. And what the Bible means is this: God wants people in His revolution who are dead to themselves, who are unresponsive to themselves. He wants those who don't respond to anything but God, who are dead to everything but Him.

That is what the Bible is talking about.

That is what it takes to belong to Christ's revolution. Jesus Christ is simply saying, "If you want to be a member of My revolution, than I demand that you give up yourself, take your attention off yourself, have nothing to do with yourself. I want you to be willing to die to your own ambitions, desires, goals, to become caught up with Mine." That is what Jesus Christ is saying.

There is no place in the kingdom of God for people who

are caught up with themselves. The name of the game is to be caught up with Jesus Christ. That's where it's at. So, the first ingredient for a successful revolution is to give yourself up to the cause of revolution.

This revolutionary writer I mentioned also said, "The second thing that every revolutionary has to have is love for the cause of the revolution above every other love in his life." During World War II when Hitler established a young people's army, he taught these young people that they were to be the backbone of the Nazi regime. Hitler also taught these young people to inform on anyone who spoke against him. One night, a teenaged boy heard his parents speak against Hitler and reported them to the authorities. His parents were arrested and thrown into prison. After a mock trial, his parents were found guilty of treason. The two parents were sentenced to execution by a firing squad. The star witness against them was their own son. He gave the orders for his own parents to be shot. That boy was taught that the Nazi regime was more important than his own parents. He was committed to Hitler's revolution.

Now obviously, Jesus Christ is not calling us to that kind of fanaticism. But Jesus Christ is saying this, "If you want to be My revolutionary, if you want Me to run your life, if you want to belong to this new order, then I demand of you that you love Me above every other love in your life." In essence this is the way He puts it in Luke 14:26 — "If any man would be My disciple, if any man would come after Me, if any man would be My revolutionist, and does not hate his mother, father, sister, brother, husband, wife, children and his own life also, he cannot be My disciple." Now by that Jesus Christ did not mean that one was literally to hate his loved ones. What He meant was that a person's love for Him is to be so intense, that all other loves in his life will seem like hatred in comparison. So if there is ever a showdown between what Jesus Christ wants out of your life and what Mom and

Dad want, Jesus Christ says He comes first. If there is a show-down between what Jesus Christ wants and what your husband or wife wants, Jesus says He comes first. If there is ever a choice between what Jesus Christ wants and what your sister, brother, or even what *you* want, Jesus Christ says He comes first. In other words, Christ says, "I demand to have first place in your life."

The problem is also this. As you've heard in the Scripture, love for God also means working out love to other people. There is no way in which a person can claim to be the disciple of Jesus Christ and not love people. There is no way a person can be a revolutionary of Jesus Christ and not care about the people around him. The sickness of our generation is that we have forgotten how to love. We no longer know how to care for each other. The very fact that America is torn with racism, division and hatred . . . the very fact that our nation has been turned upside down . . . the very fact that our cities are explosive and tense . . . reveals that we haven't learned to come together. It is indicative of the fact that we don't understand how to love.

But Jesus Christ is saying, "There is no room in the kingdom of God for people who don't know how to love." The real issue of our time is that we haven't learned how to relate to each other. It is not only a matter of race, it is a matter of people against people. White people don't know how to live with white people who are on a different social or economic level. Black people don't know how to live with black people whose thinking is different. If you go into white communities, you find upper class, middle class, lower class — and each class has little to do with the others. Another community might be separated on the basis of religion or politics. If you go into the black community you will find the "Uncle Toms" who don't want anything to do with the radicals, and the black bourgeoise doesn't want anything to do with another group. So the bourgeoise, radicals and Uncle

Toms are all clashing. No one living together. No one loving.

Every community is faced with these problems. Our solution is to learn what it means to be committed to each other. And the greatest crisis we face in America today is whether we can bring people together — whether people will ever learn what it means to love.

The love I'm talking about is not mushy, not emotional — it's a commitment. It fleshes itself out in action.

Don't tell me you love me but you can't be concerned about my welfare.

Don't tell me you love me if you're not committed to my safety.

Don't tell me you love me if you're not committed to justice.

Don't tell me you love me if you're not committed to feeding the poor and hungry.

Don't tell me you love people if you're not committed to putting shelter over their heads.

Don't tell me you love people if you're not committed to the welfare and well-being of people around you. In other words, the Bible states clearly, "How can you say you love God, that you're committed to God, whom you cannot see, when you cannot love your brother to whom you relate every day?"

The issue is simple. To be a disciple of Jesus Christ means to love Him. If you're not prepared to love Him above every other love in your life then you cannot be His revolutionary. Jesus Christ bases the whole criteria for love on the way we relate to each other. Jesus said to those people, "Depart from Me. I don't know you."

They said, "Lord, how come?"

He said, "Very simple. When I was hungry, you gave Me no meat. When I was thirsty, you gave Me no drink. When I was in prison, you didn't visit Me." In other words He based the criteria of love to Him on the way they responded to each other. Thus, there is no way by which you can say you are a disciple of Jesus Christ if you do not care for the needs of people.

You see, I know the other side of it. I used to run the streets of Harlem as a black revolutionary. And I used to rap down to the others in the community, "Brothers, we gotta get together, man. We gotta get together and do our black thing. We gotta come together and unite against Charlie because *he's* the enemy." But funny thing. Every guy whose head I busted, you know who he was? A black. Every guy I ran my blade into, you know who he was? A black. Every store I raided, you know who owned it? A black. And yet I went around saying, "We gotta get together." There is no way you can talk about getting together with each other until you become committed to each other.

Look at the political situation. We stand up in America and we say, "one Nation under God." We're not one nation. We are not together. We have Democrats against Republicans, blacks and whites at each other's throats. We have Indians and the white society now in a clash, minority groups being locked out of the system. And we stand up and claim with integrity that we are "one Nation under God." We are not one nation and the closest thing to being "under God" is that we have His name on our money. That is all. We are still divided. And this division will keep any revolution of love from succeeding.

Finally, the third ingredient listed by this revolutionary writer was: "Every revolutionary has to forsake everything for the cause of the revolution." In substance, Jesus put it this way (Luke 14): "If any man would be My revolutionary and does not forsake all that he has, he cannot be My revolutionary." That has to be one of the toughest verses in the Scriptures. Many people wish it wasn't there. There are those people who say, "Well, God doesn't mean for us to give up everything. I can follow Christ and do my thing without giving up everything." They say, "What the Bible really means is that we should be *willing to*." Check out that verse — do you see the word willing? "If any man would be My disciple and does not forsake all that he has, he cannot be My disciple." This does not necessarily mean that God expects you to go out, take the last shirt off your back and live in abject poverty. It doesn't mean He plans for you to take everything you have, dump it, and live like a hermit. But it does mean that all that you are, and all that you have, is to be totally committed to Jesus Christ — that He owns you and everything you have — lock, stock and barrel. He has the right to do with you and all that you own as He pleases. That's the whole name of the game.

You say, "But, Tom. That's fanaticism. I can't buy that kind of Christianity. I can't buy that kind of commitment where I've got to give up everything to follow God. That's fanatical. You're asking the impossible." Is it? I have a friend, twenty-four years of age, just graduated from Harvard Business school with a master's degree in business administration. He landed a job in a company with $24,000.00 a year to start. They told him it wouldn't be too long, because of his brilliant executive acumen, before he would be made a partner in the business. But one day he received a letter from the local draft board, telling him that he was being drafted into the United States Army. He took the letter to work and informed his boss that he had to quit his job "because Uncle Sam has called."

Suppose I say to you, "Listen, if that guy tells his boss he's quitting, he's out of his mind. He's a fanatic." And you say, "No, Tom. Uncle Sam has called him. It's a matter of patriotism, obedience and duty. He must answer the call."

I say, "Call or no call, he's making $24,000.00 a year . . . $2,000.00 a month. You mean he's going to give up $2,000.00

a month to go to the United States Army and make $100.00 a month? You're out of your mind."

You say, "No, Tom. He has to do it. Uncle Sam has called."

So, he goes home and tells his family he's leaving to answer Uncle Sam's call. And as he walks out the door, his relatives try to hold him. His children grab him by the pant leg and say, "Daddy, don't go." They start crying.

And I say to you, "Look, if that guy walks out the door and leaves his family like that, he's a fanatic. He's out of his mind."

You say, "No, Tom. He has to leave his family. Uncle Sam has called him. It's a matter of obedience. He has to do it, he has to go."

He puts on a United States Army uniform, and renounces all rights to civilian life. Before, if he wanted to go downtown and go to a movie, he could do it. If he wanted to eat out he could do it. If he wanted to go away on a weekend vacation, he could do it. Now he can't leave the base without a pass from his commanding officer. He can't go anywhere without permission. If the officer says, "About face," he has to turn about. If the officer says, "Forward, march," he has to march. Whatever his commanding officer says, he has to do.

And I say to you, "That dumb fanatic! He's given up all his rights to let someone else tell him what to do."

You say, "That's not fanaticism, Tom. That's obedience. That's duty. That's patriotism."

Then they ship him off to Vietnam. And his commanding officer sends him out on a search-and-destroy mission in some rice paddy and he is shot down . . . dead. And they send a telegram home to his wife and a check for $10,000.00 saying, "Your husband died in the line of duty."

And I say, "That fanatic. He gave up his job, his home,

his civilian rights, and now he's given up his life. To go out
for what?"

You say, "Tom, no. You've got it wrong. It's a matter of
heroism. He died for his country. He gave his life for a
cause."

Then I turn around and say, "Well, that's exactly what I
want to do for Jesus and you tell me I'm a fanatic."

Commitment is not fanaticism. In substance, the twelfth
chapter of Romans says: "I urge you to present your life to
Jesus Christ as a living sacrifice, acceptable to God — which
is a reasonable, normal action on your part." That's not
fanatical. In fact, you're not "normal" or reasonable until
you've made that kind of commitment. That's the whole
name of the game. Jesus Christ is the only true radical who
ever lived. He's the only true revolutionary alive.

I'm suggesting to you that most other revolutionaries are
hypocrites or at best, unable to carry out their claims.

They cannot change that system because changing the
system means changing people.

There is only one man alive in the whole universe who can
change another man. That man is Jesus Christ. The Bible
(II Corinthians 5:17) says: "Therefore, if any man be in
Christ, he is a new creature: old things are passed away;
behold, all things are become new." I'm saying Jesus Christ
is where it's at. He's the radical. He does the changing.
Systems are made up of people. You want a revolution?
You want to see the world changed? Then, very simply,
you have to begin with yourself.

How radical are you? Has Jesus Christ come to live in
you?

I'm not talking about church. Please don't take anything
I've said to have anything to do with religion or church. I'm
not preaching church or religion here. I'm talking about Jesus Christ. There are many people who, when I talk about a
total commitment to Jesus Christ, think I mean being totally

committed to some denomination, church, or institution. Let me make it clear. That is not what I'm talking about. I'm saying, "Jesus Christ, a person who's totally alive, wants to live in you." That's the issue.

So I'm asking you to forget about what church you go to; forget about whether you've been baptized; forget about whether you've been religious.

The issue is this: *Is Jesus Christ living in you?* If the an- swer is "No," then I offer you, right now, the opportunity to become *His* radical. I offer you the opportunity to commit yourself to Him.

Again, never mind religion. Hang religion. That's not the answer. Never mind the church. That comes later. Never mind the hypocrites in these institutions because God isn't going to ask you about the hypocrites. He's going to ask you about *you.*

What are you doing with Jesus Christ? Is He running your life? Is He living in you? Has He *radicalized* you? That's the issue.

Jesus Christ is the only platform from which a true radical, revolutionary program can be launched. And I offer to you the opportunity to trust Him. I offer you the opportunity right now, wherever you are, to invite Him to come into your life.

I did it. Ruthless, arrogant, bigoted, I invited Jesus Christ to come inside and live in me and life has never been the same. I'm still a revolutionary . . . with a different platform. I now have a new leader. A different cause. A different set of principles. But I'm still a revolutionary.

If you want to learn what it really means to be radical, and want your life turned on . . . to know how to live in a messed-up world with your head screwed on right, look to Jesus. I'm saying Christ is the Person who can do it. He wants to come inside and live in you. Jesus Christ says in His Word, "A person who comes to me, I will not cast out."

No person who came to Jesus Christ has ever been turned away. He won't turn *you* away.

Are you His revolutionary?

Have you given up yourself?

Can you honestly say you love Jesus Christ above every other love in your life?

Have you come to the point where all you are and all you have is committed to Him? If the answer is no, I offer you the opportunity to do it right now. If you would like to become a revolutionary for Jesus Christ — not church, not religion — just bow your head right where you are, right now, and in your own heart, in your own words, simply say, "God, that makes sense. I never knew that Jesus Christ operated at the gut level. I never knew that He was that contemporary. I never really understood that right now Jesus Christ can live His life in me. I'd like Him to run my life."

All you have to do is tell Him that. And in the Word of God, Jesus says, "Any person who comes to Me, I will not cast out." Would you like to become a member of the revolutionary army of Jesus Christ, to go out and change the world in the name of Jesus? Do you want Him to come inside by changing you first, living His life in you, forgiving you of every sin? He can give you everlasting life that no one can take away — with absolute assurance that you belong to Him and He belongs to you. He backs it up with a guarantee that once He comes in, He will never leave you nor forsake you. If that's what you want, then I invite you right now to bow your head and pray, "Lord, I don't understand it all. I don't dig it. I have so many hangups. I'm confused, messed-up, and I need You. Come into my life and take it over, run it and let me be a revolutionary for You."

And life will really begin for you, as it has for me.

3

To Change the System

One of the great issues that people are talking about today is: *How do you change the system?* Few people are naive enough to believe the system doesn't *need* changing. It does. The areas of disagreement arise in discussing how we should go about accomplishing this change.

How *do* you change the system?

How do you go about correcting a system that is obviously stacked against many groups of people?

Is it possible to salvage anything from the existing system — or must we, as many radicals suggest, burn it down?

Some people are optimistic. They say change is possible within the system. The more pessimistic revolutionaries say, "You can't beat city hall!"

But whatever the attitude, there are growing numbers of people — not just young people — who are saying the system has to be dumped in favor of something that works — and works for all people. It is obvious to them that the present world system, and present governmental systems are not working. To say that they work is self-delusion.

Even in America — where we're prone to use words like "democracy," "freedom," "pursuit of happiness" and "liberty and justice for all" — there are problems.

Not all Americans have freedom.

Not all people are able to participate in the system.

And there are some very real problems. For example, last year 43,000 people committed suicide — discovering that the system had no real answers to their problems. So they "copped out" of the system.

It is interesting to notice that the average income of the 43,000 Americans who committed suicide last year was something like $25,500.00 a year. Now a person ought to be able to get by on "25 thou." He might have to miss a couple of meals, buckle in a little bit and go on an austerity program, but he ought to be able to get by on "25 thou." But 43,000 Americans couldn't pull it off. Obviously their income, their social status and whatever else they had was not capable of helping them survive in the system.

If you talk to 500,000 American Indians you discover that vast numbers of them are not part of the system. Many of these 500,000 "original citizens" are not even free to move from one place to another as citizens. They need passes to move around in our country. And it seems very interesting that before the white man came these people occupied and owned this country. But now in America — the "land of the free and the home of the brave," there are 500,000 people who aren't really free in a country that was once theirs. They are not part of the system.

In the twentieth century, there is a large group of American people, notably young people, who are saying, "These things are wrong and need to be changed!" Some of these young people are indignant; some of them are violent; some of them have a great sense of moral conscience; some are just as oppressive as the system they want to demolish.

Some of these people differ as to method and end results, but all are committed to the fact that the system has to be changed. The system has to work for everyone. And many of them have been discovering that because they want to change the system, they have been meeting with fantastic opposition.

We have found all kinds of reasons not to hear out these young people.

"They don't act right."

"They wear long hair."

"They wear dirty clothes."

"They're not respectable."

"They are too militant."

"They use bad language."

But these young people are saying, "The system needs to be changed."

Two years ago, 15,000 young people converged on the city of Chicago in the name of trying to change the system. Of course they shook up most of us, not because they were young people. Not simply because they came to Chicago to argue politics. It was not that they came and made noise that really disturbed us. It was not even the fact that they taunted the police. What disturbed us most was that they came in the name of change.

They came to try to change something.

They came to try to reconstruct something, to produce a new order. No matter how awkward or corrupt they were, they, in essence, wanted to change something. And it is difficult for many to experience change.

Long before it was fashionable to call it revolution, young people were being disruptive. But we always wrote it off by saying, "Boys will be boys." You remember twenty or thirty years ago, on most college campuses, there used to be what was called "panty raids." Young men would raid the girls' dormitories and steal "unmentionables" as souvenirs. And when the students were caught, most administrators just laughed it off saying, "Boys will be boys."

Ten years ago young people used to tear up telephone booths to see how many people they could stuff inside one.

And we heard reports from the University of Idaho where they broke a record — five hundred young people stuffed into one telephone booth. They tore down the telephone lines, broke up the telephone booth and the telephone repairman came the next day saying, "Boys will be boys." Nothing was ever really done about it.

Yet, all of a sudden, we have become disturbed about young people of today. Not because they are disrupting. Not because they are being violent. Not because they are militant. But because they have threatened to change the system. About two months before the 15,000 Yippies and Hippies converged on Chicago, a group of 30,000 conventioneers came to Chicago. And when they hit Chicago there was more booze, more destruction of property, more prostitution, and more immorality going on in this town than those 15,000 young people could have created in a year. But no one said anything. No one became disturbed about 30,000 conventioneers who spent more money on prostitution than has ever been spent in this city in one time. But we were disturbed about 15,000 young people. Why? Because one group came to town to *change* something and the other group came merely to *buy* something.

The name of the game is "How do you change the system?" People are becoming fed up with the present system. They are saying that you can no longer hide immorality behind prestige or money. You can no longer write it off with religion.

Revolutionary forces, whether we like them or not, are at work today, saying, "The system has to be changed because it is corrupt." Now in the middle of this, we ask ourselves, "Are there any answers? Are there any real solutions?"

As I have already stated, of all the great revolutionaries and radicals who ever walked the face of the earth to change or beat the system, I am convinced that the most radical revolutionary is Jesus Christ. The Christ who leaps out of the pages of the New Testament, the Son of God who became a man, walked the face of the earth for a purpose. *One*: He came to tell us how to beat the system; *two*: He came to tell us how to change the system; and *three*: He came to tell us how to make the system work for men. You ask, "Is that possible?" If I had heard someone make this statement about Jesus Christ and His plan to change the system years ago, I would have tuned it right out. I wouldn't even have heard. Because, you see, the people who were basically talking to me about Jesus Christ were also people who were part of the system. In fact, they ran it. My difficulty was that I could not respond to their concept of Jesus Christ because He seemed irrelevant to my kind of life.

I was born in Harlem. The block I lived on had four thousand other people living there with me. In two and a half square miles around me there were one million people. Social statisticians tell us that if you took the entire population of the United States — all two hundred million Americans — and concentrated them into the five boroughs of New York City, New York, this area still would not be as congested as Harlem is right now. Now, to this overcrowding, add the element of poverty. Forty percent of the community is slums. Fifty-seven percent of the kids grow up without their fathers. Many of them are out on the streets as pimps and prostitutes long before they are fifteen years old. There is police brutality. Much of the racketeering that goes on in the community is maintained by the people who are part of the system, who speak out in the name of law and order — but who refuse to be lawful or to maintain order in the community where I lived.

Those were the ones who came along to offer me church and Jesus Christ. And I said, "No, thanks." I had discovered there wasn't too much difference between some religious institutions and the corrupt society. In fact, I learned that the institution was very much like the society. I knew that people *outside* of the church were bigoted. But I discovered there were some inside who did not believe in law and order. I knew that outside the church there was crime and disregard for human dignity, but I discovered that these also existed *within* the religious institution. And I had no way of separating the two. I said, "The society is corrupt, the church is in the society, therefore, it must also be corrupt."

When they talked to me about Jesus Christ and told me that He was the head of the church, I said there must be something wrong with Him too. So I had a problem. All the images that had ever been projected to me of Jesus Christ were that He too was a member of the system. In fact, the people who had messed up the system often used Jesus Christ to provide some kind of sacredness to the way they ran their corrupt institutions. So they wrapped Jesus and the American system up in the same bag and tried to offer me Christ and I said, "Absolutely *no way.*"

My other problem was this. The images of Jesus Christ always had Him come across looking like part of the system. He had ash blond hair, blue eyes, regular features — pretty. He looked too much like a pansy to survive in my neighborhood. My response was this. "If I am going to commit myself to a Saviour, He's got to be gutsy. He's got to be a Christ who can get that landlord off my back. A Christ who can drive brutal policemen out of my neighborhood. A Christ who can deal with racketeering and drug addiction. A Christ who can deal with rats. A Christ who can deal with slums. A Christ who can deal with bigotry, hatred, and division." He had to be tough. But the image they gave me of Jesus Christ didn't come across like that.

At a very early age I had joined the church, trying to find some answers as to how to beat the system. Joining church was easy. I just walked down the aisle to shake the preacher's hand. The church clerk took my name and address and when the choir finished singing the pastor said, "We'll now have a recommendation coming from the church clerk."

The church clerk said, "We have with us this morning Master Tom Skinner, residing at 269 153rd Street, who desires to become a member of this church as a candidate for baptism."

The pastor said, "You've heard the recommendation coming from the church clerk? What is your pleasure?"

A deacon said, "I make a motion that Master Skinner become a member of this church."

Someone else said, "I second the motion."

The pastor said, "All in favor say 'aye'."

They all said, "Aye." No one said, "No." So, they shook my hand, told me to walk by the table, pick up my dues envelopes, pay my dues every Sunday and come back on the second Sunday of next month and they would baptize me. So I joined the church. But it didn't change me. It was easy to join church, but it didn't do a thing for me. It made absolutely no difference in my life.

But I became a part of the religious bag. I soon became president of the young people's department in my church. My father was pastor. I played the game. I went to church every Sunday, went through all the motions, did exactly what everyone else did and yet every night during the week I was busting someone's head, running a knife in someone's body. I was breaking into someone's store or house. I had the game down pat.

Now you couldn't say that I was really bad, because, after all, the people I was surrounded with were no different. There were large numbers of people in my church who played the same game. The difference was, they didn't belong to my kind of gang. And they didn't do it my way. They were a little bit more sophisticated. But I was accustomed to deacons showing up a little juiced on Sunday morning. I was accustomed to men in the church running around with other men's wives. It was amusing to go to conventions and watch people register in the hotels with women other than their wives with them. I was accustomed to playing the game. I soon learned how that system worked. So I said, "Who in all the world is going to beat the system? It can't be beaten with church or religion because they're playing the same game."

I found no real answers. So I couldn't beat that system.

I tried to find something that would relate to me, something that would give me a sense of my own black dignity and pride. I turned the radio on and heard "Amos 'n' Andy." *That* was going to teach me how I could get into the system? Mistake. And so I looked for help on television. There was Rochester, Jack Benny's sidekick. He came out and said, "Yes, Boss," and "No, Boss," and they said *that was me* and I said, "No way!"

I went to first grade and they gave me a grade one reader. Thumbing through the book I tried to find something that related to me and I found nothing. They gave me a story about Dick, Jane, Sally and a dog named Spot who said, "Bow-wow." But none of this related to me. Nor could I buy the fact that "Little Black Sambo" was for me, someone with whom I could relate and identify. None of this said anything about my style of life. So I continued my maddening search to discover myself.

How in all the world do you survive? I asked. I tried the religious bit, that didn't work. I tried the educational route, that didn't work. I tried to set myself free and that didn't work. And I felt hemmed in.

I joined a Harlem street gang in my search for answers. But after much violence, much frustration, and much searching, I became confronted one night with one of the most fantastic messages I ever heard. I was told about a person called Jesus Christ. Now, mind you, I had been hearing about Jesus Christ all my life. Being a preacher's kid, going to church every Sunday, I had heard the whole thing. But I had never heard about Him in any real relevant sense. He was always a Christ who was way out there somewhere, but never a person who operated at gut level. But I was told one night about a Christ who could relate to me, where I was. This Christ was not a member of the establishment. In fact, He came to address Himself *to* the system. I discovered, not a lofty Christ, but a Jesus who rubbed shoulders with people in the nitty-gritty of life. He dared to mingle and talk with prostitutes, drunkards, and people of ill repute. And it was very interesting that this is why the people who were most opposed to what He said, did and stood for . . . those who were most intimidated by His radicalism, were those in the religious power structure of His day. The greatest accusation brought against Christ was that He rubbed shoulders with sinners. But more than antagonizing members of the religious system by His associations, Jesus stirred things up by the radical things He had to say. He dared to call one group of establishment hypocrites "a generation of vipers," and "filthy graveyards." He challenged them to show a sense of morality. And more than the radical things He said were the radical things He did. He came to create a revolution, to change the system.

And I discovered that the day in which Jesus Christ lived was in many ways similar to my time. In those days the Jews were being exploited by the Romans. The Romans had moved into Jewish territory and said to the Jews, "We are here to run things and if you keep things cool, nothing will happen to you." A Roman could walk up to a Jew and say, "Look, carry my bag for one mile," and the Jew was compelled to carry his bag. The Roman troops paraded up and down the Jewish neighborhood, exploiting Jewish people, raping Jewish women. No different. It was the same system.

But there arose, on the streets of Jerusalem, a revolutionary named Barabbas. And Barabbas began to rap to his people,

"There is only one way to get that Roman honkie off your back — burn him out!" So Barabbas and his band of guerillas burned Roman homes, jumped Roman soldiers on the streets, and killed Roman soldiers whenever they could do it without great risk. Before long Barabbas and his band of revolutionaries were creating havoc in the community, trying to beat the system.

Finally, they arrested Barabbas and charged him with insurrection, murder, and anarchy. And they locked him up.

In the same streets of Jerusalem was another revolutionary. Another radical. His name was Jesus. He had no guns. He had no tanks. He had no ammunition. He had no band of guerillas. He had no military program. You need to understand something here. Jesus Christ would not have taken issue with Barabbas at the point of the problem.

Barabbas said, "Look, the Roman system stinks. It's militaristic, it's racistic, it's oppressive. It doesn't work for all the people. The Romans are only out for themselves. They're not willing to give justice to all people. That system has got to go."

I am certain Jesus Christ would have agreed with him. He would have said, "Barabbas, you are absolutely right. The system *does* stink. It *is* militaristic, it *is* oppressive, it *does* lack justice, it *does* lack love. There is *not* freedom for all people. Barabbas, you are absolutely right!"

A large number of people in American society today believe that Jesus Christ would have tried to preserve the system. They firmly believe that Jesus Christ would not, in any way, have anything to do with trying to change the system. In fact, they think Christ would crack down on the hippies and rebels of our time. Many of these people put Jesus on the side of the system. They say, "Boy, if we could just get people to accept Christ we could save the system. If we could just get people to accept Christ we could put the lid on the riots and trouble. If we could just get people to believe in God we can preserve our great American heritage." *I'm not so sure that Jesus Christ is interested in preserving a corrupt heritage.* I'm not so sure Jesus Christ is interested in preserving something that does not offer freedom and justice and liberty to all men everywhere.

So, Jesus Christ would have fundamentally agreed with Barabbas. He would have said, "Barabbas, you are absolutely right." And I think Jesus would probably agree with many of the radicals of today — even groups like S.D.S. and Yippies — as they tell how corrupt the system is. You know why? Because most of these kids are the sons and daughters of those who run the system. They know how corrupt it is. Jesus wouldn't argue with them. When Black Panther leaders Bobby Seale or Eldridge Cleaver stand up and talk about the oppression, militarism, the institutionalized and individual racism in American society, there is no way you can disagree with them, because as they diagnose the situation, they are absolutely right.

The point of disagreement comes where it did with Jesus Christ and Barabbas — not in the diagnosis of the problem — but in the handling of the solution.

Jesus would have said, "Uh, uh. You have to have a whole program. If you're going to change a system, you'd better have a program as to how you're going to replace it. Barabbas, you're making one great mistake. You are assuming that because you are oppressed you are somehow more moral than the oppressor. Barabbas, I am telling you that there is no difference in morality between you and the Romans. There is no difference between a corrupt Indian and a corrupt white man. There is no difference between a corrupt black man and a corrupt white man. They are both corrupt. So, you have to change people first. Now, Barabbas, I have come, not only to change the system and not only to change the people who are oppressors, but I've come to change the oppressed. Because you see, you can never really set the victim free until you set the oppressor free."

So Jesus came to change the system. Thousands came to hear what He had to say. And they responded to Him. Before long He was putting homes back together, lives back together, and people started finding their identities. Dead people came alive, deaf people heard, the blind saw, and before long people began to change in such dramatic ways that the whole Roman empire began to shake beneath the message of a Man who had no gun, no tanks, no armies. He just stood up with a fantastic rap and a strong case in the name of His Father, and taught people that they could become radicalized by God. And He shook the Roman empire. He became dangerous. A man who starts changing the system is dangerous. You see, Barabbas was dangerous because he wanted to change the system. Jesus is dangerous because He, too, will change the system. The difference is in style.

The question is not whether there is going to be a revolution, it's a question of who's going to lead it. I want you to understand that I believe revolution in our country is inevitable. There *have* to be changes. There has to be some kind of revolution. There is no way to stop it. The question is, what kind of a revolution? *We do have an option.* We can decide between Barabbas and Jesus. Either one of them will change the system. One will do it the wrong way and one will do it the right way. Either way the system will be changed. It's up to you to decide who will do it.

Jesus said, "I've come to radicalize men into the kingdom of God, men who will go out and change the system by being new men in an old world . . . men who are going to be a breath of fresh air in a stale desert . . . men who are going to be water in dry land . . . men who are going to be light in darkness. I've come to produce a new order of men who are attracted to Me." Now any time a man starts talking that strong, there are going to be problems. When a man starts shaking up the religious, political, and social system, the people *in* the system feel they have to stop him. During Jesus' day there were two groups in the religious establishment, the Pharisees and the Sadducees. The Pharisees had nothing to do with the Sadducees. The Sadducees had nothing to do with the Pharisees. They hated each other and were always arguing with each other. They were always struggling for power in the temple, trying to see who would be top man. Then Jesus came along and began to threaten both their systems and denounce them both. Strangely the Pharisees and the Sadducees suddenly got together. Now they had a common enemy. They conspired to have Jesus locked up because He was "dangerous."

So now there are two radicals in jail, Barabbas and Jesus. Around the festivity of Jewish Passover time, the Roman governor, trying to keep things cool in the Jewish neighborhood, gets up in front of the Jews and says, "Look, I've got two revolutionaries in jail. And you know how much I love you dear Jewish people. I've always loved the dear Jewish people. In fact, some of my best friends," says Pilate, "are Jews. And not only that, the guy who ran my bath last night was a Jew. I even had lunch with one last week. So I have nothing against you dear Jewish people. And to show you how much I appreciate you dear Jews," Pilate said, "I'm going to release one of them. I'm going to let one of these radicals go. And I'm going to give you the choice to decide which one of them you want. Now over here I have Barabbas. He's an insurrectionist, anarchist, murderer, and liar. He's been burning the system down. Do you want me to release him? Should I let him go? Or over here I have Jesus who claims to be the Son of God. I've examined Him and I can't find anything wrong with Him — other than the fact that a few dead people are now alive, a few blind people are seeing, some deaf people are hearing. I understand He fed a few thousand people with a few loaves and fishes at a social welfare program.

But I can't find anything wrong with Him. Now should I release Him or should I let Barabbas go?"

And with one voice they cried out, "Give us Barabbas! Give us Barabbas!"

"We will not have That Man rule over us."

Now your question is, "Now why in the world would they want Barabbas? Barabbas is the guy who was going to destroy the system. Barabbas was going to burn them out. Barabbas was going to kill them. Why would they want Barabbas?" It's very simple. If you let Barabbas go, and he starts another disturbance or another riot, you can always call out the National Guard, the federal troops or the Marines to put his thing down. All you have to do is push a few tanks into his neighborhood and you can squash whatever he's up to. You can find out where he's keeping his guns and raid his apartment. You can always stop Barabbas. But the question is: *how do you stop Jesus?* How do you stop a Man who has no guns, no tanks, no ammunition, but still is shaking the whole Roman empire? How do you stop a Man, who — without firing a shot — is getting revolutionary results? They figured there's only one answer — get rid of Him. They made the same mistake people have made down through the history of man. They thought you could get rid of the idea by getting rid of the man from whom the idea comes. So they said, "We can get rid of Jesus. We don't want Him to rule over us."

Barabbas would never really ask to run your life. Barabbas would exploit you, but he wouldn't ask to run your life. Jesus would ask to run your life. Jesus would ask for the right to rule over you! And that's the problem. Men would rather be enslaved to tyranny than to let Jesus rule their lives. They would rather be exploited than let Christ determine their lives. So they said, "Give us Barabbas."

They took Jesus, mocked Him, beat Him, and forced Him to carry a cross up to a place called Calvary. They laid Him down on that cross, and drove spikes through His hands and feet. While they were doing that, soldiers dug a hole in the ground, picked up the cross, and dropped it in the hole so that the spikes ripped through His hands and flesh. They stood there and mocked Him, spat at Him and crucified Him. And they little realized that as they were nailing the radical, revolutionary Jesus to the cross, they were also killing the Son of God.

Long before the foundations of the world, God decided His Son would come and be put into the hands of angry men, nailed to a cross for the sin of all humanity. On that cross, Jesus Christ died not only for the sins of the radicals. He died for the sins of the militants. He died for the sins of the "Uncle Toms." *He died for the sins of the whole world.* Nailed to that cross, He shed His blood to forgive us of every sin we've ever committed.

He died on that cross. They took Him down, laid His body in a tomb, and sealed the stone over His grave. Then they wiped their hands and said, "That's one radical off our backs. He won't disturb our temple any more. He will never bother us with His talk of morality and conscience any more. He will never again share His revolutionary ideas that shake up the world. We are rid of Him! He is done with! Now we can go back to business as usual: stepping on people, raping and ravaging. He can't bother us any more!"

Three days later Jesus Christ pulled off one of the greatest political coups of all time. He rose from the grave, saying, "All power is given unto Me in heaven and in earth. And with this power, I'm prepared to radicalize men for God. I'm prepared to make revolutionaries and radicals for the kingdom of God."

Now doesn't that make sense?

Jesus Christ says, in John 6:37, "The person who comes to me I will not cast out." The Bible also says, "He that believeth on Christ (the word 'believe' means to trust) will have everlasting life." The Bible teaches that any person who invites Jesus Christ to live in him, Jesus will come in, take up residence in that person and begin to live His life through him. Think of it — the power of God, the life of Christ, living in him.

Jesus Christ came to break the system, and make it work for all men. He came to put in a new system called the kingdom of God. He is truly a radical, a revolutionary who is concerned about the needs of men. And any person who receives Christ and His power into his life will also become radical. He can go out into a system in the name of God, directed by godly principles and the Word of God, to *change the system!*

Make no bones about it, I'm a militant.

Make no bones about it, I'm a revolutionary.

Make no bones about it, I believe in being radical.

The difference between my militancy, my radicalism, or my revolutionary concepts and the concepts of other people who claim to be revolutionaries is that my whole revolutionary platform is built on what God says in His Word. It's disciplined by the Word of God and by the Holy Spirit. I responded to that kind of Christ. I heard for the first time in my life that Christ was prepared to come inside and live in me, and that it wasn't just "pie in the sky." It wasn't just looking forward to the hereafter. It wasn't just a matter of a passport out of hell into heaven. Christ was interested in the world I live in now with my two feet planted on the earth. He impregnated the common clay of my humanity with His life and sent me out to affect other men.

I discovered that Christ was concerned about hungry people. Christ was concerned about poor people. He was concerned about people who were being mistreated. Christ was concerned about freedom and justice. He was concerned about all the things it takes to set men free. For those who took no interest in the needs of men, He had words of judg-

ment. Jesus said they would be banished to everlasting punishment. And they replied, "Oh, no, Lord, we're religious
leaders. Lord, did not we preach in Your name? We sang
in the choir. We were deacons. Lord, we did many mighty,
wonderful works in Your name."

Jesus Christ said, "Depart from Me, you workers óf evil.
I don't know you. I have nothing to do with you."

I'm saying being a religious leader, a deacon, a trustee, a
choir member . . . simply going to church . . . being a Bap-
tist, Methodist, Presbyterian, or whatever, does not plug you
into God. There are going to be more people in hell who
are religious than prostitutes or drunks.

Jesus came to ask us to forget the system and forget about
our trust in our religious deeds. They're no good, He says.
He wants us to commit ourselves to Him, saying, "In the
system you will have pressure. But be of good cheer, I have
overcome the system. I have beat it. I have smashed it. I
have made it possible for you to live in it. You can be lights
in a dark world."

The question is, do you want to respond to Him? Remember, I'm not talking about a pansy Christ. I'm not talking
about an American Christ or Russian Christ or any other
narrow view of Him. I'm talking about the Christ who is
Lord of heaven and earth, and who — in spite of that —
chooses to call you to Himself. So you see, the reason I
don't belong to most other so-called radical or revolutionary
groups is that they are not radical enough. Jesus Christ is
where it's at. You want to have a revolution? Come to Christ
and He'll revolutionize your life, first, then your world. Will
you respond to Him? Will you join Him to beat the system,
to overcome the world? You can be God's revolutionary in
a mixed-up, confused, racist, militaristic, oppressive society.
You can go out and set other men free so they can get
plugged into God and learn to be the vehicles through whom
God expresses Himself. Do you want to be a part of that

system? Do you want to be a part of that revolution run by God — with His system, built on justice, freedom, and liberating people? The Bible says, "Whom the Son has set free is free indeed."

I invite you to respond to that Christ. Hear a new sound, discover a new Jesus. Let Christ turn you on. I invite you to come to Him, right where you are, right now, to take Him at His Word. He's the only revolutionary who lived, died and rose again. He's the only revolutionary who has never lied to His followers. Will you come to Him? Will you give Him your life? You will be forgiven of every sin you ever committed. Your nature, which is now independent of and defiant to God, will be replaced with the nature of Jesus Christ. You will be given everlasting life, that is the life of Jesus Christ forever. No one can take it away. You will be liberated from all guilt of the past. Your guilt will be wiped out. You will stand in the presence of God just as if you'd never sinned. And then, Jesus Christ, without any help or assistance from you, just your availability to Him, will send you out in the world to set other men free. That's what it's all about.

Now if that kind of Christ makes sense to you . . . if that's the Christ you want, if you can dig that kind of Jesus, I ask you to bow your head right where you are, right now. And in your own words, simply pray, "Lord, I'd like to trust You. I'd like to invite You to live Your life in me. I'd like to become a radical of Jesus Christ." The moment you invite Him to come inside and live in you, Jesus Christ, the Son of God, *will come in.*

You say, "But Tom, I don't feel anything." Don't be looking for a feeling. Faith has nothing to do with your feelings. The Bible says, "He that believeth (not he that feeleth) hath everlasting life."

Just ask Jesus Christ to come inside and live in you. And He will.

4

America, Your Days Are Numbered

Professionals from all walks of life are telling us that the human race is in trouble. Biologists, ecologists, psychologists, sociologists, economists and political experts are all united in this diagnosis of trouble. Of course, God — through His Word — has been telling us for a long time that mankind is in trouble. Unfortunately, men have not listened or responded.

Another thing we have considered is the fantastic age in which we live. This time can best be described as revolutionary because of all the changes we have seen, and will see, in our society.

Change is inevitable if society is to survive, say these experts who have been observing human history. What kind of change is coming?

Within the next ten years, there will be more changes than all the alterations that took place from 1901 to 1970. We will see fantastic growth and development, similar to what we have already seen. We are told that sixty-five percent of all the products on the market today did not exist five years ago. We used to talk about a generation as being about twenty years; now we talk about a generation being only five years. Young twenty-one-year-olds, people considered radical by the older generation, are considered square by their six-teen-year-old brothers and sisters.

Now in the middle of all this, the question is: Is there hope? Is there hope for the human race? Is there hope for America? Is there hope for us as individuals? We are being told, day after day, that we are in a crisis period. For example, a leading biologist at Harvard University says that at the rate that we are polluting the air, we have no more than ten years of healthy air left in America. Someone put it this way, "It seems as if the world is being judged." Many people agree. They say time is running out. That attitude is summed up by many of our young people.

It was assumed ten years ago when we talked about the drug problem in America, that we were talking basically of poor people. So, very little was done — maybe there was some legislation passed to drive drug pushers out of some of the classier neighborhoods — but there were absolutely no concerted efforts made to curb the problem. Today other classes of people are disturbed about drugs — mainly because their own young people are taking drugs. The young people who are "tripping out" or "copping out" of the system today are not just poor kids from the ghetto. They are the sons and daughters of senators, governors, and congressmen. They are the children of businessmen and factory workers — sons and daughters of those who *own* the system.

After investigating and analyzing why young people today are "copping out" of the system, many tell us it is this matter of time running out. Young people firmly believe the world, in the hands of their parents, will not last too long. They think the human race is about to destroy itself, and although they want to do something about it, the attitude of many young people is "eat, drink and be merry, for tomorrow we die."

As I think of that, my mind goes back to a situation that developed centuries ago. This situation is very relevant to our hour and I would like to share it with you. The context of the story is that a war had broken out and part of the population of a particular nation had been cut off from the rest of the nation. There was a man who was second ruler in the kingdom. This man, Belshazzar, met one night in his palace with one thousand of his lords and threw quite a bash. And as the party went on into the night, there was much boozing, revelry, drunkenness and lewdness. In a drunken stupor, King Belshazzar asked one of his servants to go to the temple of God to get certain gold and silver vessels which had been dedicated to the service of God. The man was to bring them back to the palace so the people could drink from them. And as the party lasted into the night and the drunkenness and lewdness increased, the top politicians and leaders of the kingdom were just about out of it.

Suddenly there appeared poised above one of the walls of the palace a hand — without an arm — and it began to write on the wall. The banquet guests at the palace who were in this drunken stupor sobered up suddenly. A hand, not connected to an arm, was writing on the wall. The king looked at the writing but couldn't decipher it. So he called for some of his lords and they couldn't decipher it either. He rang for the minstrels, ministers and interpreters to try to figure it out. Nothing happened. The search went around the kingdom to find someone to decode this handwriting not known to anyone in the palace.

The name of Daniel, a man of God, came up. He was brought to decipher the writing on the wall. And he translated it for them. He said: *God has numbered your kingdom and He has finished it. You are weighed in the balances and you are found wanting.*

"God has numbered your kingdom and finished it. You are weighed in the balances and found wanting." If ever there were words that were appropriate to America in this hour, I believe these words are so. With the intense conflict and immorality, with the total mess that we are in here in the twentieth century, I believe God is saying the same thing to America.

God is saying the same thing to Chicago, New York, Philadelphia, and to major cities across America. "I have numbered your kingdom, I have finished it. You are weighed in the balances and you are found wanting."

For a number of people who link God only to the American system, that is heresy. Unfortunately, there are people who believe that God has settled only in America, and heads just the American system. They tend to believe that God is on their side, that "in spite of our problems, we are not really so bad, because after all, America was founded by godly men and built on godly principles."

Unfortunately for these friends, God is no more committed to one nation than any other (unless it be the Jewish nation). He is the God of heaven and earth, looking at us and weighing us by certain standards. I believe, based on what is happening in America today, the words of God to King Belshazzar apply to us: "I have numbered your kingdom. I have finished it. You are weighed in the balances and you are found wanting."

Now let's try to get a grasp of the standards by which God judges people. We could begin by being a little negative and discussing the standards by which God does *not* judge men. God *does not* judge men by an educational standard. If God had judged King Belshazzar by educational standards, the king would have passed with flying colors. Obviously a man of royalty, he had been groomed from early childhood for his role of leadership. He was taught by the best tutors. He was made aware of all the philosophy, history, and mathematics known in his time. It was not a matter that Belshazzar or any of his thousand lords who "partied" with him that night were not educated. They were informed people. Unfortunately, God does not weigh people in the balance of education. God has other standards by which He measures a man.

If America were to be judged by its educational awareness, we would pass with flying colors. We are the most informed generation in the history of the world.

God does not judge men by how wealthy they are. If so, Belshazzar would have passed this test with flying colors, too. Obviously, he was a wealthy man, with all the gold and silver of the kingdom at his disposal — a man who had everything he needed to live. But still God judged him. God said, "Your kingdom is numbered. I have finished it. You are weighed in the balances and found wanting."

If America were to be judged on its economic wealth, or its materialism, we would pass with flying colors. We are a wealthy nation. Most people in our country eat well. The average income is up. Many people understand what it means to have economic and material security.

Incidentally, I think it is interesting that our material wealth hasn't solved our problems. It hasn't taught us how to relate to each other. It hasn't ended war, poverty, racism and division. It hasn't destroyed militarism. It hasn't brought an end to a messed-up society.

I think it is also interesting that the young people who are "dropping out" of the system today are the young people who come from a system where there is financial security. The young people who are becoming the most radical in the twentieth century are no longer the poor kids. Those seeking revolution and reform on college and university campuses and within the political system of our country are young men and women who come from *wealthy* homes. They understand that wealth alone doesn't give a man a reason to live.

No, I submit to you that God does not judge nations nor people by their economic security. Whether you are rich or poor, God will not judge you by your economic status. God has another scale, another standard, by which He judges man.

Neither does God judge man by his religious persuasion. Belshazzar was obviously a religious man. He believed in a God somewhere. No doubt he had his own private minister. Yet, in spite of his religious inclinations, God still judged him.

America today is a "religious" nation. We are a people who believe that God is "up there somewhere" but somehow we haven't plugged in to Him. Most Americans go to church. We even have God's name on our money, and we salute the America flag as "one nation *under God.*"

In spite of all this outward religious show, it is obvious that we have excluded Him from our lives. For many of us, God is dead . . . rendered thus by our lack of action and response to Him. We live day by day without ever bothering to consult God. I believe the words of God are appropriate to us: "You are weighed in the balance and you are found wanting."

During the days of Belshazzar there was a special kind of scale used. It was called a balance. If you went to the market to buy five pounds of potatoes, they took a prefixed weight and put a five pound weight on one side and on the other side they added the potatoes. Naturally, when you put the prefixed weight on, the scale went lopsided. But as you added potatoes, the scale started balancing. When both sides were level, you knew there were five pounds of potatoes and you were getting a just amount.

The scale about which God was talking to the king was similar. On one side of the scale were all the demands of a holy God. On the other side sat King Belshazzar and all his kingdom — and the scale didn't balance. So God said, "The scale is lopsided because you don't balance out to My standards, because you don't measure up to what I've called men to be. You are weighed in the balance and are found wanting. Your kingdom is finished. I'm doing it in."

Now, maybe this is the time to discuss what the standards of God *are*. What are the measurements by which God deals with men? You'll find them listed very clearly in a single biblical passage — in what has become known as the Ten Commandments. These are the words by which God judges nations, communities, institutions. And I ask you to see yourself as an individual, as a member of an institution, as a society or whatever else you represent. Put yourself on one side of the scale, put the demands of God on the other side, and ask yourself, "Do they balance out?"

Listen to how God starts off. He says, "You will have no other gods before me." Now most people say, "Well, you know, that rules me out. I'm not a pagan. I'm not a heathen. I don't go dancing around idols. I believe there is a God up there somewhere." But many people mistake what God is saying. When He talks about having other gods, it is not necessarily graven images to which He is referring. Rather, He is talking about anything in your life that is the most important thing to you. That is your God.

Religion is defined as that which a person feels to be of ultimate value. Whatever is the most important thing in your life is your God. Think about it — what is the most important thing in your life? For some of you, your home is the most important thing. That's your god. For someone else, it might be his car. That's his god. For someone else, it might be his job. That's his god. For someone else, it might be his children. That's his god.

In other words, whatever is the most important thing in your life becomes your god. And God is simply saying: "If you do not want to be judged — if you want the scale to balance out — I demand that you have no other gods in your life. I ask that nothing else in your life be as important to you as I am. I want to have first place in your life, to be Lord of your life."

We are a nation that worships the god of materialism, the god of money. Money has become so important to us in American society that we're willing to lie and cheat and kill for it, all in the name of gaining the dollar. I was talking to an executive of one of the leading electronic firms in our country some time ago. And he said to me, "You know, Tom, every time one of our planes is shot down in Vietnam, there is a slight glee at the table of our Board of Directors, because we have the contract to rebuild those planes. And while we are Americans and want to win the war in Vietnam, we're still just a little bit excited every time one of our planes is shot down because it means another contract for us."

That's what the love of money has done to American society!

We've come to the place where human rights are no longer important, people are no longer important, *lives* are no longer important. It's money. And many of our young people are rebelling against the system because we have become a nation that worships the god of money and materialism. We are to the point where we are no longer committed to human rights.

A struggle for equality has been taking place in our nation. Americans watched TV as riots and disturbances also took place. And as these people watched their television screens and read in their newspapers about the disorders, they missed the whole point completely. These were not hoodlums on the streets, but frustrated young people, not necessarily out to tear down the system, but many of them legitimately reacting because they felt locked out of the system. They felt the world was stacked against them. They looked at a world of institutionalized racism and saw no hope, and in their frustration they took to the streets. It never bothered the American people — watching all this on TV — that a number of these young people lived in rat-infested homes. It never disturbed them that the landlords in these neighborhoods didn't provide services for their buildings, or that the sanitation department didn't make as frequent garbage pickups in those neighborhoods as they did in others. Nor did it disturb the American people that those kids and their parents paid twenty-five percent more for food at the supermarket in their neighborhoods than other communities. It never bothered the American people that the police in those neighborhoods were brutal, nor that those kids didn't receive justice and did not have security or their rights.

Instead, people missed the point completely and said, "We've got to protect property rights. We've got to protect property values." We became more committed to property rights and property values than we did to human rights, values and lives. Why? Because we worship the god of materialism, and we bow at the shrine of money.

We've been willing to do anything at the cost of the dollar. The so-called pollution problem in America would not exist today if American industry had not been as greedy as it has been in the past years. If our politicians had been more alert to the needs of the people than to the needs of the business community, America would not be facing the environmental crisis it faces today. God looks at America's millions who have turned their backs on Him to worship at the shrine of materialism and money and security, and His words are: "I have numbered your kingdom. I have finished it. You are weighed in the balance and found wanting."

Another standard by which we can measure ourselves is a word in that same Scripture passage as the command above. This second commandment says, "You shall not kill." Most people will back off from that. They say, "That excludes me. I'm not a murderer. I've never run my blade into anyone's ribs. I've never shot anyone. I'm a law-abiding American citizen."

But listen — Jesus Christ put it this way: "It has been said of old that you shall not commit a murder. I say to you, anyone who hates his brother has already committed murder." In other words, as far as God is concerned, you don't have to shoot a man down or physically kill him. If you bear malice, hatred, bigotry or prejudice against someone, according to the Scriptures you are guilty of murder. God does not place the emphasis so much on the action as on the way a person thinks. The Bible says, "As a man thinks in his heart, so is he." God judges people by how and what they think. God judges people by their attitudes.

If you want to correct the way a man behaves, you must correct his thinking. A couple of years ago, I decided that in order to keep up with my very enterprising associate, Bill Pannell, I'd better learn how to play golf. But as I got out on the course, I was pretty bad. I decided that maybe I'd better spend a little money and take a few lessons from someone who knew how to play the game. My problem was, I'd go out, address the ball, and eventually hit it, but it never quite went in the right direction. If the ball was supposed to go one way it ended up going the other way. So my instructor began to inform me about my problem. He said I was swinging the golf club the way I would swing a baseball bat. And you can't swing a golf club the way you swing a baseball bat. If you do, as any golfer can tell you, it is bad news. My instructor said, "Tom, your problem is that you are thinking like a baseball player and not like a golfer." So he spent time trying to change the way I was thinking. He knew that once he changed the way I was thinking, it would be easy to get me to swing correctly.

"As a man thinks in his heart, so is he."

That's why Jesus Christ said, "I am not as disturbed about what you do as I am about the way you think."

"As a man thinks in his heart, so is he."

That is the problem today — we are killing each other with hatred, prejudice and bigotry. And in my opinion, there is probably no nation on the face of the earth as immoral as America in terms of human relations, brotherhood and commitment to each other.

You say, "Tom, that's not so." Well, if that's not so, why

do people have to constantly go around eulogizing America, reminiscing over our "godly" past, those "great days when America stood for something"?

My friend, those days were basically no different than the days in which we live now. Our country has always been filled with hatred, violence, and revolution. We've never been able to get along. But the problem is that today we are more intensely divided than ever before.

Our country was *not* founded on godly principles by godly men. If you check out your history, you will discover that in the early days when the colonies were formed in America, the British emptied their jails, and shipped the criminals to America to help form our colonies. They were not necessarily founded by only nice people.

You say, "Yeah, but George Washington prayed at Valley Forge and Ben Franklin opened the first Congress in prayer." It is interesting to check out the theology of George Washington and Ben Franklin. You will discover that they didn't necessarily believe in a personal, real God who could live His life through men. They were not committed to Jesus Christ who died for men's sins, who rose again to live in them. If you want to check out these men, all you have to. do is count Washington's slaves . . . or read Franklin's personal biography of the number of prostitutes he left behind when he visited Paris — not to mention his hanky-panky in Philadelphia. So you see, these were not necessarily godly men.

I do not mean that they were not committed to good principles. They were. I do not mean that they did not have noble ideas. They did. But they were no more moral than any other Americans. And if you think that America is going to escape the judgment of God by creating a myth that America was *founded* by God, you are making a mistake. God has numbered our kingdom, and we are found wanting. We are weighed in the balances. We haven't learned how to live together. God is simply saying: "You don't know how to get along with people; you have violated a commandment of God. You are guilty of murder." It is all too evident in the racism and hate which flows in the streets of America, pitting black against white, society against society, religion against religion.

The *Wall Street Journal* recently ran an article reporting that there has been an intense resurgence of violence and bombings of black churches in the South. There has been a revival of murder and hate because large numbers of people now feel that the government is easing up on its program for racial justice. They claim Washington wants to go back to bondage and periods of segregation. This attitude is giving rabid segregationists the feeling that they can come back into power. Once again there is the conflict and intense feelings of hatred that we thought were past in the 1950's and early 1960's. But here they are again, seeping through in the 1970's. It seems we are moving back a century, past the period of reconstruction, making the same historical mistakes that we made a hundred years ago. Our young men and women, both black and white, are becoming so disenchanted with the American system and its inability to bring people together, they feel that there is no other answer but to go out and destroy the system. Yes, we are facing problems and we have trouble in America. We haven't learned how to live together and it is resulting in murder.

As long as we are excluding any number of people from the mainstream of our society, we are committing murder. And God simply says: "I have judged you. I have weighed you. I have numbered your kingdom. I have weighed you in the balance and you are found wanting."

Shall we judge ourselves in the light of another of God's commands? "You shall not commit adultery." Most people, when they think about adultery, think strictly in the narrow sense of sexual immorality. It means that, but it means much more. The word adultery is taken from the Latin word *adult-*

erate, which means "to corrupt." The Bible teaches that when you take something God has consecrated — something dedicated to the service of God — and use it for your own personal, immoral ends, you are committing adultery.

That night King Belshazzar committed adultery when he sent to the temple and had those consecrated gold and silver vessels brought back to his own palace to use in "boozing it up." Whenever you take anything that is committed to God, and use it wrongly, you are corrupting it. You are committing adultery.

Our young people are seeing through our false morality. We stand up and face our young people and we tell them to be pure and moral, yet wc go out and create for them a society that is totally immoral. One young girl put it this way, "My father is an advertising executive. He tells me he wants me to be pure. He tells me he wants me to be moral. He tells me he wants me to grow up a virgin, and yet *he* can't produce one ad without selling sex with it. When he draws a picture of a car, he has to put a sexy girl in the car. If he wants to sell a cigarette, he puts a sexy girl holding it. He sells sex — day in and day out — and then tells me to be pure."

Young people are saying, "We don't want any part of that kind of morality."

Until we are able to produce morality for our young people, and set personal moral examples for them, we can't demand that they be moral.

We lie to our young people. We tell them to stay pure, and then do just the opposite ourselves. We teach by example a philosophy that there are no rules, no standards, by which God judges men. And as a result, we have produced another immoral society.

Our young people today are no more immoral than any generation in the past. It is just that many are more honest and more open about it today. These young people are simply saying, "We are no longer going to play any games." We have created a society which has corrupted our nation. We are committing adultery by taking our natural resources, our people, our youth and wasting them for our own greedy or impure uses. God is saying, "I have judged you. I have weighed you. I have found you wanting." We are corrupting something that God wants to use for Himself.

The lives of our young people are being corrupted by our dishonesty. Adultery has to do more than with just sexual immorality. But God knows that *that,* too, has become a great issue in American society. Americans worship the god of sex. But God is saying, "I've numbered your kingdom. You are found wanting."

Another of God's commands says, "You will not steal." Most people think stealing is taking something from someone else. And most of us say, "I don't really do that. I'm a nice person. I don't steal."

Some of us steal like hoodlums and some of us steal in a much more sophisticated way. We are told by *Harvard Business Review* that last year more than $13 billion was stolen in government and industry. The question is: Who stole that money? Obviously not poor people. Obviously not hoodlums. Obviously not the people we would lock up. Basically, the thieves were the respectable people, the "nice people." They were the people who would go to the polls and vote to have "law and order."

They were the same people who used to tell me that if I didn't go to bed at night, or stop making noise, the "boogie man" would get me. They lied to me about that — and about a jolly old man called Santa Claus. Of course, if I had been sharp, I would have been able to figure out that game about Santa Claus. I should have known that no white cat was going to be in my neighborhood after midnight.

Well, I suppose I could forgive the lies about Santa and the "boogie man." But the problem was that they lied to me in different — more harmful — ways. When I went to school, they lied to me — inferring that I didn't count as they excluded me from their books. They lied to me about my history for they told me that the most I could look back to was the fact that my ancestors were ignorant slaves. They never told me that white men "discovered" America, with hundreds of thousands of Indians already living in this country.

You know, it's like walking to a parking lot with you and spotting a sharp, $6,000.00 automobile and saying, "Man, that's a good looking car."

You look it over and admire it, too. Maybe you say, "You know, I'd really like to have that car."

So, I turn to you and say, "You can have it."

"What do you mean, I can have it?"

"Right, man — all you have to do is go over there and 'discover' it. That's all."

We have lied. Young people in America are disturbed with the way some government leaders have been lying to us. They say our leaders have deceived us about the war in Vietnam, the political system, even about the way things are being done in our country. Although these young people are not necessarily any more moral than their parents, they are saying, "We are tired of being lied to. We are tired of false stories and 'credibility gaps.' "

The *Wall Street Journal,* one of the leading newspapers of the Establishment, recently said something like, "There are over thirty million stockholders in America. Everyone can own a piece of American society. Everyone can have a piece of American business. There are thirty million stockholders." But the article somehow avoided telling us how much stock those thirty million stockholders owned. Many thousands of them owned maybe two shares of AT & T each, or one share of GE, one share of IBM, two shares of DuPont and so forth. The truth of the matter is, when you boil the whole thing down, *4.7 percent of all stockholders in this country control more than 85 percent of all the stock!*

And they tell you that all people can have a piece of American business. In reality, just a handful of people in American society control the country's economic and political wealth and power. In many ways democracy is a myth. "Everyone participates, everyone can have something to say, everyone can run the American system," they tell us. Yet, the political leaders, without consulting you or me, sit down and they decide on who they will run for president, governor, mayor — even dogcatcher! They come out with their choices and ask us to decide between the two.

God simply says, "Look, don't play games with me. I see America. I see the way you are. You have been weighed in the balances — you have been found wanting. I have numbered your kingdom. Your game is up. I have weighed you in the balance and the balance is lopsided. You are found wanting."

Now the issue is: *how do we balance the scales?* How do we set the record straight? If we can't measure up in any areas, how do we reconcile men to God? How do we get men back to God so that He is first in importance in their lives? How do we learn to be honest with each other?

How do we stop lying?

How do we come to the place that we can relate to each other?

How do we stop having attitudes of murder against one another through hate, racism and bigotry?

How do we eliminate a system that's immoral and corrupt — and come up with one that works?

God has only one answer. The Bible says the heavens and earth were searched for someone to balance the scale, for one who could sit on the other side of the scale and balance God's demands. No one could balance the scale. There was neither man nor angel who was capable of doing it. And finally the Bible tells us, that God Himself decided to do something about the situation. In John 1:1 we read, "In the beginning was the Word, and the Word was with God, and the Word was God." Later in that same passage it says, "And the Word became flesh." God came to earth as a man, Jesus Christ. For the first time in the history of man, God manifested Himself in human flesh. God, through His Son, Jesus Christ, decided to come and sit in our place and balance the scale.

Jesus Christ walked the face of the earth sinless — never committing injustice, never hating, never committing immorality, never placing any other gods before Him. He was the only man that ever lived who lived up to the standards of a holy God. The Bible declares that because He lived up to the standards of a holy God, He was worthy to bear our sinful nature in His own body. He was worthy to die in our place, to be made sin for us. Jesus was worthy to experience the hell we deserve. The Bible declares He was nailed to the cross, crucified for us, shed His blood to forgive us, rose again from the dead to live in us. And the Bible declares, as a result of His resurrected life — because he is now alive — He is prepared to live His life in anyone who dares to trust Him.

The Bible declares, "Therefore if any man be in Christ, he is a new creature." The scale starts balancing. When God is on one side and you are on the other, things are lopsided — until Jesus Christ joins you and balances the scale. So, you see, living up to the standards of God is not something that you can do.

If you listened very closely to the Scriptures that we've just cited concerning the Ten Commandments, you will discover that every one of us is guilty of breaking one or more of God's commands. The Bible says, *"All* have sinned and come short of the glory of God." It says, "There is none righteous, no, not one." None of us in this world has lived up to the standards of a divine God. And yet the Bible declares, "The soul that sinneth, it shall die." And "The wages of sin is death."

The Scriptures declare that there is no hope for the sinner apart from the hope in Jesus Christ.

You cannot live up to the standards of God, but Jesus Christ can live up to them. Instead of going out and breaking your neck to be holy, trying to be a Christian, trying to measure up, God says, "Why don't you give up? Why don't you relax? Why don't you stop trying to balance the scale? My Son has already done it. He has met all My holy demands and when you ask Him to come inside and live in you, He will do it — He will balance things."

God declares that the moment you invite Christ to live in you, you stand in His presence justified. The word justified can be defined as *"just as if I'd* never sinned." If you commit yourself to Jesus Christ . . . if you invite Him to come inside and live in you . . . the Bible declares that God will accept you, just as if you'd never sinned.

Many of you want to change the system. You're fed up with hypocrisy. Some of you are fed up with the whole church scene, with religious leaders who haven't told you the truth. Some of you are fed up with American myths. Let me offer you one hope right here. Jesus Christ is the liberator. He won't lie to you. He will level with you. He will set you free. I therefore invite you to Him. I invite you to trust Him. I invite you to commit yourself to Him.

America faces the judgment of God, so if you're putting your trust in America you're in bad shape. If you're putting your faith in democracy, capitalism, socialism or communism, you're in trouble because all systems are judged and found wanting. Some of us think it's just communism or socialism in trouble. No. It's every system run by men. They will all be brought down, because they are all the works of men. God is going to come to establish His own order. That's why I'm hanging with Jesus. And I invite you to Him, to trust Him right now. I invite you and dare you to come to this Person, Jesus Christ, who is alive from the dead, who wants to

balance the scale in your life, who wants to forgive you all
your sin. He is the only One who can make God's scale balance.

If you are prepared to make that kind of commitment, to
trust a radical Jesus who came to destroy the systems of men
and to replace them with His own system; if you are prepared to be forgiven of every sin you've ever committed, then
invite Jesus to live in you.

The Bible says in John 3:36, "He that believeth on the
Son . . . (the person who puts his trust in the Son, who
stakes his life on the Son) will have everlasting life." And
everlasting life is the life of Jesus Christ that no one can take
away.

Do you want to see the system changed? Do you want to
escape the judgment of God? I challenge you to understand
that the system is already judged, the world is judged, America is being judged. And if you want to escape that judgment, come to Jesus Christ, get plugged in to Him and let
Him do His thing in you. Let Him run your life. There is
no other hope.

I'm not talking about church. Going to a church cannot
save you. I'm not asking you to become religious. That can't
save you. I'm not asking you to join anything. That can't
save you. I'm inviting you to come to Jesus Christ. I'm asking you to let Him come inside and live in you.

If that's what you want, then bow your head right where
you are and simply say, "Lord, I recognize that I am a sinner. I recognize that the scale is not balanced in my life. I
recognize that I've come short of Your standards. I'm sorry.
I repent. And I now invite You to come inside and live in
me to balance the scale. I now ask You to forgive me and
to accept me just as if I'd never sinned."

Christ has come, lived and died for you. Christ is risen from
the dead and is prepared to live in you right now, to run your
life — to make you a "new creature." He is ready to balance

the scale in your life so you escape the judgment and become His personal representative to a messed-up world.

The moment you invite Jesus Christ to come inside and live in you, the Bible says He will.

5

The Ultimate Ambition

Psychologists tell us the greatest need men face today is to set goals and ambitions for themselves, then to have the motivation or drive to go after those goals. We are also told that people who don't set goals usually develop poorly in terms of learning how to live.

After interviews with scores of people, psychologists noted that large numbers of people stated that they wanted more out of life. They wanted achievement. These people who were interviewed were the most secure and had the greatest amount of emotional and psychological stability. But they wanted to achieve. They yearned for accomplishment. They wanted to set goals for themselves and be ambitious enough to accomplish them.

I graduated from high school in New York state. There we had what is known as the New York State Regents Examination. To graduate, a student must pass a series of state examinations in history, English, mathematics and whatever foreign language he had taken. Perhaps the most important examination was the one for English, because part of it consisted of writing an essay, for 30 out of 100 points. There were five topics from which to choose. The year I graduated, one of the topics we were asked to write on was, "What do you consider to be life's greatest ambition?"

If the psychologists are right that people must have ambition and achievement in order to have a sense of success and well-being, what is the greatest achievement a man can reach out for? What is the greatest goal? What is life's greatest ambition?

My mind goes back to the words of one of the most exciting, colorful people to live during the first century. His name was Paul. In a very provocative passage in the Bible he talks about what he considers to be the greatest ambition a man can have. I would like to examine the words of this man, Paul, and see how they fit into our own personal lives.

What is your greatest ambition? What is your greatest desire? What conditions must exist in your life before you consider yourself successful?

There are some people who say, "Well, I'll be a success when I've accumulated so much money."

"I'll be successful when I've achieved a particular position in my company or industry."

"I'll be successful when I've gained prominence or attention."

What is life's greatest ambition? What conditions ought to exist in your life to determine whether you are really successful? Notice my "translation" of the words of Paul in (Philippians 3:4-11): "If it is right to have confidence, I certainly should have more of it than anyone else. I was born from the people of Israel; I was circumcised on the eighth day; I was a member of the tribe of Benjamin. I was, in fact, a full-blooded Jew. As far as keeping the law was concerned, I was a Pharisee and you can judge my enthusiasm for the Jewish faith by my active persecution of the church. As far as the law's righteousness is concerned, I don't think anyone could have found fault with me. Yet, every advantage I had gained, I considered 'loss' for the sake of Jesus Christ. Yes, I look upon everything as loss compared with the overwhelming gain of knowing Jesus Christ, my Lord.

For His sake, I did — in actual fact — suffer the loss of everything. But I considered it useless rubbish compared with being able to win Christ. For now my place is 'in' Him and I am not dependent upon any of the self-achieved righteousness of the law. God has given me that genuine righteousness that comes from faith in Christ. How changed are my ambitions. How different are my goals. Now I long to know Christ and the power shown by His resurrection. Now I long to share His suffering, even to die as He died, so that I may perhaps attain as He did, the resurrection of the dead."

Let me give you the background of this guy. He studied at the feet of one of the most philosophical men of his day, a man by the name of Gamaliel. And if Paul had been alive in the twentieth century, he would have had a string of degrees behind his name — a Ph.D. in philosophy, a doctorate in theology — at the very least. Probably he would know a little bit about economics and political science. He was bilingual; he spoke both fluent Greek and Hebrew. And, of course, Paul was very religious. He was a Pharisee, which meant that he fasted a couple times a week, prayed three times a day, gave ten percent of all of his earnings to the church, and never missed a "Sabbath-go-to-meeting."

Paul had social status. He was born from the people of Israel in the tribe of Benjamin, which was quite prestigious — like making the social register today. He could trace his family heritage back to Abraham — so Paul took great pride in who he was.

Yet, with all his religious and political authority, with his economic security, educational background and tremendous intellectual ability, Paul says, "All the things which were gain to me, those I count loss for Christ; in fact, I count everything loss that I might know Christ better. In fact," he seems to add, "I count it all garbage, that I may be found in Him, not having my own righteousness which is of the Law, but that I may have the faith which is in Christ."

Now what prompted Paul to make a statement like that? Was he mentally and psychologically off balance? Either he had lost all his marbles or Jesus Christ was the most fantastic person he had ever met.

What is it that causes a man who has wealth, economic security, popularity and status to stand up and say, "I count all of it garbage that I might win Christ. I count all of it garbage that I might have a new kind of ambition, a new sense of achievement, a new sense of success."

What is it that causes a man to make a decision like that? Well, let's begin by considering those things that he considered *loss*. He starts by listing his family background, his family heritage, as loss, as garbage. Paul was a man who was a Jewish "blue-blood." During the day in which he lived, people took great pride in their family heritage. Those who were born Jews, who could trace their family heritage back to Abraham and were members of one of the twelve tribes of Israel, took great pride in the fact that they were Jewish "blue-bloods."

But there was another kind of Jew. He was born a Gentile, born outside of the Judaic circle, but at one point in the course of his life he became converted into the Jewish religion. And while most Jews accepted him, they never did so fully. They said, "It's nice you've been converted into Judaism. It's nice you practice the Jewish religion, but you're not like us. You can't trace your heritage back to Abraham. You can't prove that you're a Jewish 'blue-blood.' You don't really have Jewish blood in you. That makes us just a little bit better than you are."

There was a third kind of person in this day. He was born outside of the Jewish circle and remained so. He was known as a Gentile. And, of course, Gentiles were really scorned by these people who were taking great pride in who they were.

So, Paul sat down and wrote a letter to them. He said, "Look, if anyone has any reason to boast and have confidence in himself, I have — in fact, more than all of you. I was born a Jew from the tribe of Benjamin. On the eighth day of my birth I was circumcised. I've obeyed all the Jewish laws. I fast, pray three times a day, I give ten percent of all my earnings to the church, and go to services every week. I observe all the laws, rules, traditions and customs. If anyone has any reason to be proud, I do." Yet when it comes to his family background, Paul says, "I count my heritage as garbage that I might win Christ."

Family background is important to many people. I remember during my college days, there were students who would spend hours in the school library, going through genealogy books which trace family trees. And every now and then there would be a big yelp from the library as some guy would discover that his great-great-great-great-great-great-cousin had come over on the Mayflower. He was excited about the fact that he could trace his family heritage all the way back and prove that he was an American "blue-blood." Being able to trace his family heritage was very important to him. It gave him a sense of pride, dignity, and a sense of belonging.

Even in many places today, there are still those old, staid families who take great pride in their background. And when little Suzy comes home from college, she announces to Mom and Dad that she has finally discovered the guy with whom she would like to spend the rest of her life. She's all excited, she's in love; she's met this wonderful and exciting guy. But when all the excitement cools down, Mom and Dad, very cool and calculatingly, ask, "And what is his last name? What does his father do?" It is very important to them that she marry into the right family; that she marry into the "right kind of blood."

So, you see, there are many people concerned that whatever "noble strain" they have might be preserved. The apostle Paul says, "That is no longer my hang-up. As a result of my commitment to a very radical Jesus Christ, I have discovered that the moment one commits himself to this person, Jesus Christ, he becomes a member of the royal family of God, which puts him in the best family stock in all the world." And he adds, "I therefore count all other relationships as garbage by comparison."

Some of the tremendous social problems we have in American society today can be traced to this whole business of blood strain. Everyone wants to have the right name, come from the right heritage, right family, right background. It means nothing but prejudice. Even in American society today, much of the troubles regarding racial prejudice and bigotry have started with the so-called preservation of what some call "special blood strains." You hear people talking about the struggle for an equal, integrated society, and they say something like, "Well, you know I'm not so much bothered about integration as what it will lead to. Because integration will lead to intermarriage, and intermarriage will mongrelize the races."

That kind of talk is a cop-out. It's a shallow cover-up for simple prejudice. These people are really afraid that integration — even intermarriage — would un-do what some call a "great heritage." Unfortunately, there are no longer any real great heritages. There are no longer any "pure" strains or "pure" races to preserve. So this whole business about "preserving great heritages" is a false issue. It doesn't work. If it did, somewhere in the world you would find a race of people with the same eye color, the same skin color, and the same hair color. But they don't exist.

When black people were brought to America most of them were pure Negroid. Less than eight percent of all black people in America are now pure Negroid. There are similar patterns in the other races as well. The problem is, this whole business about "pure strain" and "pure heritage" doesn't hold water if you really want to maintain integrity.

The apostle Paul says, "I am no longer hung up about pure strain. I'm no longer hung up about heritage. I am no longer hung up about family name. I've discovered something else. I've committed my life to Christ." Paul is talking about commitment to a Christ who wants to live His life in you. Jesus Christ walked the earth for 33½ years . . . a man who was unique in the history of men. He was the only man who ever lived His life in total dependency upon the God who sent Him.

Jesus Christ never made a move without His Father. Because He lived His life in total dependency upon His Father, He was the most radical, revolutionary man who ever lived. By virtue of His perfection, He was the only man in the human race capable of assuming our role, our punishment for the demands God has placed on humanity.

Paul tells us that Christ died on the cross to do away with our independence, that He shed His blood to forgive us of wrong acts and thoughts, and rose again from the dead to replace our sinful natures with His own life. "Therefore," Paul says, "anyone who receives Christ into his life becomes a son of God. He becomes a member of the royal family of God. And by virtue of becoming part of God's family, he develops a relationship with God that supersedes any other relationship on earth." And Paul is saying, "I have a sonship with Christ and one with men. I count my sonship with men as garbage that I might retain my sonship with Christ."

That attitude also has something to do with one's sense of security. We are all aware of the intense racism in our society. Millions of people, who have been victims of institutionalized as well as individual racism in American society, grow up psychologically damaged, with a great sense of insecurity about themselves. The psychological damage done to people who were victims of racism made them insecure, made them feel inadequate, that they did not have status. That's why there has been the tremendous move in the last ten years to reverse the whole concept of individual dignity, especially in the black community. For the first time, there was a whole new breed telling us that "black is beautiful," that "black is where it's at." But it must go far beyond that. Merely pinning labels on yourself and trying to "psyche" yourself up into a feeling of dignity does not necessarily give it to you. You must accept what is already yours.

It used to disturb me that people would not fully accept me. I used to be really shook about the fact that I could not live in any neighborhood I wanted to, or that certain people did not want to rub shoulders with me or have anything to do with me socially. It was not because it was an infringement on my dignity or my personal freedom. I was shook because I felt inadequate. Somehow I felt that these people who stepped on me thought they were more adequate and I had to break my neck to try to prove to them that I was really as good as they were. But as a result of my commitment to Jesus Christ, since I became a member of His family, I do not have to go out to struggle to prove that I am adequate.

I now know who I am.

I am God's son.

No one can take that away from me.

I'll never forget when this whole truth dawned on me. A college administrator at the school I was attending called me into his office. I was achieving fairly good grades and he was quite excited about it. This dean said to me in his most patronizing tone, "You know, I am so glad that you have come to this college to make something of yourself."

And I said, "Sir, I would like you to know that before I came to this school, I was already somebody. I didn't come here to be made somebody."

In essence what Paul is saying is, "Because of my commitment to Jesus Christ, and because I am a member of His family, there is no struggle on my part to prove that I am somebody. I *am* somebody. I am God's son. That puts me in the best family stock in all the world."

So when I get disturbed about people who don't want me to move into certain neighborhoods, it is no longer because I want personal acceptance. I am now disturbed because it is a matter of law and of my own constitutional rights. It's a matter of justice. And when I get shook up, I'm shook up because I'm fighting injustice. I'm no longer shook because those people don't consider me to be their equal. My attitude toward those folk is very simple. I'm a member of the royal family of God. If you don't want to rub shoulders with royalty like me, that's your problem, not mine.

Paul counted his family heritage as loss that he might win Christ. But he also counted his *religious* heritage loss. Now doesn't that blow your mind? He counted his religious heritage as worthless. Here was a man who went to religious services every week, a man who prayed three times a day. Here was a man who, twice a week, turned his plate over and didn't eat anything — fasting as a spiritual exercise before God. Here was a man who took ten percent of his entire income and gave it to the temple. Paul was a religious man, if ever there was one, a man committed to all the religious customs. And yet he says, "Those things, including my religious heritage which could be gain for me, which could give me prestige, I count as loss for Jesus Christ."

There are those who would argue with me and accuse me of being anti-church or anti-religious because I say Paul accounted his religious heritage loss. But let me remind you that religion is defined as that which a person feels to be of ultimate value, and he is taking action in the light of it. Whatever is the most important thing to you, that's your religion. Simply because you belong to a religious group does not mean that you are plugged in to God. It does not mean that you have a relationship with Christ.

There is a difference between being Christian and being

religious. Most people are religious. Most Americans go to church. For some people, church is the most important thing in their lives. That's their religion. But it's important that we define what we mean. There is *Church* (capital "C") and there is *church* (small "c"). Anyone can belong to a church. You can join easier than you can join the Elks or the Masons. I joined very easily. I was a member of the church with the small "c." I still hadn't gotten plugged in to God. I still didn't know the first thing about Jesus Christ. I still didn't know the first thing about what it meant to be Christian. I was now a member of an institution and that's all.

Eight years later, I was sitting down mapping out strategy for a gang fight, while listening to my favorite disc jockey. The program was interrupted by an unscheduled gospel program and for the first time in my life I heard the truth about Jesus Christ. And the truth was so radical and Jesus Christ so imposing, revolutionary and contemporary that I committed my life to Him. I invited Him to come inside and live in me. At that moment I became a member of the *Church* (capital "C").

The word *Church* means " 'called out' group of people." The Church is made up of a group of people who have trusted in Jesus Christ and who fellowship together. That's the Church. I'm a member of that Church. I'm a member of that body as a result of my commitment to Jesus Christ. So obviously, as a member of Christ's "called out" group — or Church — I am not against churches. I am a churchman. I'm a minister of the gospel. I'm a minister of the kingdom of God. But I'm here to tell you that if you think that putting your name on a church roll, or getting baptized will get you into the kingdom of God, you are wrong.

The apostle Paul had been playing a religious game. He had been going through all the motions. It was all a game. And I'm simply saying, there are people in the twentieth century who are also playing religious games. They know the language, the words, the customs and traditions. They know how to go through the motions. And, sadly, there are a few religious leaders willing to exploit people with the institution, and to let people go on playing games. But I refuse to be a part of that game! I refuse to play it.

Let us be wise enough to know the difference between religion and Christianity. The difference between Christ and the institution, between the Church and church. They are not the same. A Christian is anyone who has made himself available to Jesus Christ and who allows the radical Christ to come inside and live His life through him. Now if Christ is living His life through you, that makes you Christian. If you tell me you're Christian because you've joined the church or because you've been baptized or because you sing in a choir, then you are misinformed. You are mistaken. The Bible makes it clear that a Christian is a person who has invited Christ to live in him. There are many religious people, many people in American society who go to church; there are people who know all the hymns, prayers and all the right words — even the ritual and ceremony — who have never really met Christ. I'm simply calling those people to repentance.

Paul recognized that being religious was not enough to plug a man in to God. He said, "Not only did I think I was religious, I thought I was sincere. So sincere, in fact, I went out to persecute and kill people who called themselves Christians." Paul thought he was doing God a favor. When the crowd was stoning Stephen, one of the first early Christians, Saul of Tarsus held the coats of those who stoned Stephen, thinking he was doing a righteous act. Saul was so religious and so committed to his religious way that he thought he was helping God by killing off those "radical Christians." But then something happened to Saul of Tarsus. He discovered Jesus Christ and became Paul. He rejected his religious heritage in order to "win" Christ. If you're not plugged in to

Christ and you're going to church, you're just playing games. You can't truly be a churchman until you know Jesus Christ.

Paul also counted his economic security as loss that he might win Christ. And in America, we no longer measure a man by his character, integrity, or morality. We measure him by what he has accumulated, what kind of house he lives in, what kind of car he drives, and what kind of clothes he wears. In short, we measure him by his bank account, no longer by his integrity or character.

Even within religious circles today we are to the place where we measure success in terms of material principles rather than spiritual principles. We hear people say, "He has just been promoted to president of his company. He's now making $75,000 a year. *The Lord is really blessing him.*" And, of course, the implication is that if you haven't been promoted lately and you aren't making $75,000, maybe God isn't doing anything for you.

There is another illusion abroad among many people today. We have been hypnotized through TV and other media to think of the large glut of material goods as necessities. We see this fantastic materialistic world coming at us via the TV tube — and all this great accumulation of goods and products. Most of us know that these things are not part of every household. But many people cannot make a distinction between this fancy world and the unreal world of materialism. They see all this and want it, and the advertisers feed these desires until those who want the goods they see on TV somehow feel that they have been left out of the system. We have created a hunger and large numbers of people say, "We want in." They don't realize they have been hoodwinked by Madison Avenue to believe that the accumulation of material goods is going to bring psychological security and emotional happiness. It doesn't.

It is interesting to note that, according to psychological tests, the most unstable, the most phychologically insecure group of people in America are not the poor, but middle and upper middle class Americans. Let me give an example. If I wanted to move into a neighborhood where the homes cost $10,000 (which gives you an idea of what the homes must be like), I would have no problem regarding skin color. I'd have no problem buying a home where the homes cost $10,000. No problem at all. And, I wouldn't have a problem if I had the money and wanted to buy a $200,000 home. No problem. But if I decided to settle for a home costing between $25,000 and $40,000, I'd have all kinds of problems. Because you see, middle America consists of the most insecure people in American society. More suicides come from this group than any other. More people are receiving mental treatment from this group than any other. The children dropping out of the establishment come from these homes. These are all people from economically secure homes. But they still don't have any answers. They have discovered that material security alone doesn't help put a man together.

The apostle Paul says, "I've also discovered that." He says in the Bible, "If I'm a son of God then I'm also an heir of God and a joint-heir with Jesus Christ." He is saying that "I am related to Jesus Christ to inherit everything that God has, which makes me the richest person in all the world." The Psalmist David wrote, "The earth is the Lord's, and the fullness thereof. The world and the people that dwell therein." Now if the "earth is the Lord's and the fullness thereof" and I'm connected to Him, *then it's mine, too!*

The Bible says to those people who have trusted Jesus Christ, "My God shall supply all your need, according to his riches in glory." Now that's not just material need. That's psychological needs, human needs, the need to be loved, the need to be cared for, the need to achieve, the need to be recognized, the need to have power, the need to choose, all the needs we have as human beings.

Jesus Christ says He wants to supply our needs. So you

see, as far as God is concerned, *the issue is not how to make a living, the issue is how to live.* Any man who learns how to live can always make a living.

That's the problem in our society. *Our society doesn't know how to live.* So what do we do? We send kids to college today for what reason? To learn how to make a living.

The young man asks, "Dad, what's life all about?"

"Son, life is going to school and getting an education."

"What for, Dad?"

"Well, so you can get a good job that will get you good pay, and make it possible for you to buy the right home in the right community, make the proper investments in the right stock securities and bonds."

"Why, Dad?"

"Well, so that when you retire, you will be able to retire comfortably."

"What for, Dad?"

"So when you die, son, you will leave an estate. That's what life is all about."

So we send our kids to four years of college to learn this — to learn how to make money and get their dinner. Ridiculous! I could take you to the jungle and show you gorillas. You will never see a gorilla worried about how to make a living. He probably eats more in one day than you do in a month, and yet, I've never heard of a gorilla starving. But, the day you send a gorilla to school to learn how to make a living, you're in trouble.

The issue is *first, learn how to live.* If you learn how to live, it's no problem to get food to eat. That's the least of the problem.

The problem in American society is to teach people *how* to live. *We don't know how to live.* The apostle Paul is saying: "By virtue of the fact that I am connected to Jesus Christ and that I'm an heir of God and that I'm connected to Christ to inherit everything that God has, I can now count everything else as garbage. Because I've got it made. I know who I am. I know what God is all about. I know that God is going to meet the basic needs in my life. Now I can put my attention to going out and achieving. I can go out and make the system work for other people."

Now, I don't want you to think I'm saying that simply because one is committed to Christ and all of his individual needs are met, that he doesn't have to become involved in the struggle for justice for those people who are not having their needs met because of racism, bigotry, hate or lack of constitutional law. The reason I've become involved in boycotting a supermarket chain store in my community is because many of these stores charge more for food in my neighborhood than they do in other communities. People in my community can't afford to pay those kind of prices, so I boycott that store because it's a matter of justice. *And wherever there is injustice, as a member of the family of God and a joint-heir with Jesus Christ, it is my duty to go out and fight it.*

The final thing that Paul listed as "loss" was his social status. *Social status.* Man, more people are hung up on social status than you can ever dream of. That's the name of the game. Political cronies exercise a struggle for power, a struggle for recognition, a struggle for social status.

Who's going to be the big boss?

Who's going to divide up the pie?

That's always the question. Because we are hung up with social status, the city is explosive, the nation is explosive — because people don't understand what it means to live. Everyone breaks his neck trying to belong to a certain group of people.

"I can't associate with him because he doesn't belong to the right social group. If I'm seen with him, my friends over here might not like it. So in order to be accepted by my friends, I had better turn my back on him."

The people who need status are insecure people. And our

insecurity causes this great struggle for power, recognition, and status. But the apostle Paul says, "God has relieved me from the struggle for status. Not only am I God's son, not only am I a joint-heir with Jesus Christ," but, he says in Ephesians, "I am seated together with Jesus Christ in heavenly places." That means I — as a Christian — am on the highest social level of all the world. *I swing with Jesus Christ and Company.* I belong to Him and, as a result of belonging to Him, I operate from the position of influence and status. Paul is saying, "This is the greatest social group you can belong to. When you belong to this group, you are 'in.' This is the real 'in crowd.' I'm all the way up here with Jesus Christ in heavenly places! For me to be accepted by a group down on earth, I will have to come all the way down from where I am and break my neck trying to be accepted by a group that is inferior to the one I already belong to! And I'm not about to come down."

You see, once you get in that kind of secure position then you are in a position to move. You are in a position to motivate. But many of us, because of our insecurity, feel intimidated because we measure status by things, by social position, by economics, by external things. We become intimidated by the things a person *has.* But God never judges a person by the things he has.

God judges a man by his character, by his spiritual life, by what he is inside. That's why the Bible says, "As a man thinks in his heart, so is he."

Because of my commitment to Jesus Christ it is no longer necessary for me to go out and struggle for social recognition. I don't need it. Recognition by a man won't help me feel secure. Many people haven't discovered this yet. They feel they need the recognition of other people to be secure.

As long as you need the recognition of other people to be secure, you can always be manipulated by other people. If the man who's feeding you — your body or your ego — is the man who makes you feel that you are somebody, then you always have to play his game to feel like somebody. Jesus Christ has liberated me and provided for me personal security. I do not need the recognition of people to feel that I am somebody. He has liberated me from being manipulated by that man. That's why the Bible says, "Whom the Son has set free is free indeed." He has not only liberated me spiritually — freed me from the power and penalty of sin — but He has liberated me from the need to be manipulated. He has liberated me from being oppressed. He has liberated me from the need to have to play someone else's game to feel a sense of recognition.

I'll never forget how often I observed this as a kid in the church where I grew up. I watched insecure people in my neighborhood who were psychologically damaged as a result of institutionalized racism. Because of their need to "be somebody," they often went out of their way to do certain things. In one of the early churches my father pastored, some dear lady in the congregation had given one hundred dollars and no one listed her name on the program. She was ready to tear up the whole church because no one recognized her for the gift she gave. Here was a woman who was insecure. She wanted recognition and hoped that by giving the money someone would stand up and praise her for her action. Because she had been so psychologically scarred and damaged, she needed someone to say, "We recognize you."

The apostle Paul is saying, "If you can come to this place where you can see yourself committed to the Son of God, letting Christ do His thing in you, Christ will make it possible to produce in you an emotional, intellectual and spiritual security, where you won't have to play any games to feel recognized." That's why Paul counted his social status as loss, as garbage — that he might win Christ. When you get liberated from the need for social status it makes it possible for you to tell it like it is and be honest with people. It makes it possible for you to tell the truth, because you no longer are intimidated by anyone. That's what Christ wants to do in your life.

I'm talking about a gutsy, contemporary, radical Christ who wants to live His life in you. Christ in you and you in Christ, going out into the world to do His thing. That's what Paul is saying. I want to be found in Him, doing His thing. He says, "I don't want to be found in Christ having my own righteousness." In other words, he says, "I don't want to be a cheap imitation of the Christian life." There are many people playing games with God. They give the impression that Christianity is a game, with actors on a stage acting it all out.

In some religious circles, I get the impression that everyone is fooling each other. One group is fooling the other; the other group knows they are being fooled; this group *knows they know* they are being fooled, but they go on and play the game.

Paul says, "I don't want to play that kind of game. I want to be found in Christ. Not with my righteousness, but with His. Instead of me trying to be a Christian, I want Christ to be a Christian in me."

Let me illustrate it this way. There are some people who believe that the Christian life is carrying around in your pocket a bunch of rules and regulations — and you keep them close by. And the rules say, "don't do this," "stay away from that," "don't touch that," "don't look at that" and "don't go near that." In this "game," everyone goes out and tries to live up to the rules and they end up making neurotics out of themselves. They wear themselves out trying to adhere to all the rules and regulations. *Don't, don't, don't, don't, don't, don't, don't, don't, don't, don't, don't!* And if you manage to keep ninety percent of the "don'ts," they say you're a Christian.

Paul says, "Get out of that bag! That's not what the Christian life is all about. The Christian life is not you trying to be a Christian, because you can't do it. The Christian life is not going out and breaking your neck trying to be a Christian. Jesus says, "Why don't you just invite Me to live in you. I will come in and be a Christian in you. Instead of you trying to be a Christian, I will produce it for you. That's the Christian life."

Jesus Christ wouldn't get hung up on some of the things some religious people get hung up about. Jesus wouldn't go around measuring how long your sideburns are or how long your hair is, and whether you wear a crewcut or an Afro. God isn't hung up on that. God wouldn't go around with a tape measure, measuring the length of your sleeves or the length of your skirt. God isn't hung up on that.

God says, "Look. Commit your life to Me. Let Me do My thing in you and I will take care of every detail. Let Me run your life, and give you direction and the power to achieve." That's what it means to know Christ, to be found in Him — a radical Christ who wants to change your life.

If that makes sense, here's what I'm going to ask you to do. Right where you are, right now, simply pray, "Lord, that makes sense to me. I've been busting my head trying to be a Christian and now I've discovered I don't have to try to be one. Christ will be one in me. So I give up; I quit."

Simply say, "All right, God. I now give You the right to come inside and live in me. I'm prepared right now to give You my life so You can provide the emotional, mental and spiritual security I need. I want to become Your son, a member of Your family, connected to You to inherit everything that You have. And give me the power to be a Christian instead of me trying to be one. Lord Jesus, come into my life and live Your life through me."

That is the first step in really learning how to live!

6

It's Ability That Counts

Because of the changes occurring in our world today, people are discovering they have to make major adjustments to survive. I've already mentioned that the changes in our world are so rapid and fantastic that the next decade — 1970 until 1980 — will bring about more changes than all that took place in the past seventy years.

Marketing experts tell us that sixty-five percent of all the products on the market today did not exist five years ago. That's how rapidly the world has changed. More and more we are being told that this is an age of skill and specialization. People who want to survive in a technological society have to be highly skilled and highly trained. People have to have *ability*. Great stress is being placed upon the word "ability" today. If you want to move ahead, you have to have ability and be trained.

It makes sense, therefore, for us to go to people who are skilled and who have ability. If you want someone to teach you to fly an airplane, perform surgery on you, or even service your automobile, you seek out someone who knows what he is doing.

But people are asking even greater questions today. In spite of the great advances in technology, medicine, and the many other areas that make it more convenient for Americans to live, there seems to be very little skill applied in the area of *learning how to live together*. You've heard it said many times — we are the nation that put man on the moon, yet we can't seem to develop a society where we are at peace with each other. We haven't been able to bring an end to war, hate, hunger, poverty, racism and bigotry.

Let me illustrate it this way. An airplane pilot is a skilled man. He gets inside his plane which weighs some 184,000 pounds, and carries 150 passengers, whose average weight is something like 180 pounds. Each passenger puts 40 pounds of baggage into the cargo compartment. Then the crew fills up that plane with thousands of gallons of gasoline. The pilot then starts up the engines of that huge plane with its load of tons of fuel, passengers and cargo, and moves it away from the terminal onto the runway. He will pull back the throttle with practiced precision as the plane moves down the runway and those hundreds of tons pick up speed. Twenty-eight seconds after the jets have revved up, that plane is traveling 180 m.p.h. and lifts off the ground. In a matter of minutes it is 33,000 feet in the air, cruising at 600 m.p.h. And the pilot has absolute control of that huge piece of technological wizardry called an airplane.

About 150 miles out of Los Angeles, he decreases his power and slowly brings that plane down from 33,000 to 20,000 feet, then 15,000 . . . 10,000. He decreases the power to 400 m.p.h., then 300, 200 and finally, as he begins his approach to the runway in Los Angeles just a couple hours after take-off in Chicago, he slows down to 125 m.p.h., glides down on the runway, and makes a beautiful landing. About 15 seconds later he revs his jets and brings that plane to a complete stop and guides it into the terminal. The pilot has absolute control of the plane. Yet, if you walk up to him one minute after he gets out of the cockpit and curse him out, he won't be able to control his temper. Why? Simply because man hasn't been able to control the most important thing in his life, himself. Man has absolutely no control over himself.

Man is also learning that with all of his technological, scientific, medical and educational achievements, he cannot control hate, bigotry, malice or war. He cannot bring an end to the problems that beset mankind. So the human race is in a vast search for someone who has the ability to do something about the human problems of our time. The question is, "Is anyone able to bring people together?" Is there anyone who can solve the identity crises of our times, who can teach us how to live together? Is there anyone who can give us the power to survive as a people, to be the kind of men and women God intended us to be?

For an answer I turn to the Scriptures, the only authority from which I can discover God and His program. There is no other way I can "dig" God except through the Bible. And as I read, I become convinced that Jesus Christ has the unique ability to help put people together.

Some people get a little disturbed when you mention Jesus Christ. I can understand their problem. When I'm talking about Jesus Christ, I'm not talking about religion. Please understand that. When I talk about Jesus Christ, I'm talking about a person, not an institution. I'm not talking about stained-glass windows, steeples, or a church building. I'm talking about a *person,* Jesus Christ.

The Bible says Jesus Christ is God who became man. Jesus was the only person who lived His life in total dependency upon God, the Father. No other man in human history ever lived without sin, without alienating himself from, or acting independent of, the life of God. Jesus Christ, who could have exercised His own will, set aside His own prerogatives and became subject to the will of the Father who sent Him. So you can see why Jesus Christ is the most radical, revolutionary, "gutsy" individual to ever walk the face of the earth.

He lived a perfect life. The Bible also declares that He

came to earth to show men it was possible to live a kind of life that related to God — a life that would liberate men and set them free. Jesus Christ was radical in the human sense of the word — that is, He came to change the system, He came to "buck the tide" of opinion of His day. He came to move across the mainstream of political, economic, religious and social corruption and immorality of His day. But the Bible declares that He came to do something else.

He came to offer to men the unique ability only He could provide. What kind of ability does Jesus Christ have? What makes Him different than other great religious leaders who have lived? After all, there were men who came to start all kinds of other religious movements. Buddha, Mohammed, Confucius and other great religious leaders also had noble sayings, ambitions, as well as excellent moral and ethical principles. Now what makes Jesus Christ any different than the rest? Why should I commit myself to Him? What is unique about Jesus Christ?

The Bible states the unique thing about Jesus Christ is that He has ability. The ability He offers us is the ability to become the kind of men and the kind of women God intended us to be when He first made us.

The first thing the Bible says about His ability is written in Hebrews 7:25: "Wherefore he is able also to save them to the uttermost (completely) that come unto God by him, seeing that he ever liveth to make intercession for them."

A lot of religious people go around using the word "saved." Before I became a follower of Christ I didn't have the slightest idea what they were talking about. I used to ask "saved from what?" You know, "What are you talking about, I need to be saved? I'm not drowning." I always pictured someone out in the middle of the ocean, trying to stay above the water, hollering for help.

Or, when someone said to me, "Tom, you have to be saved," I thought of the money I was putting in the savings

bank every week. What do you mean I have to be saved?
Saved from what?
Saved for what?
Saved to what?
What do they mean when they say I have to be saved?

Webster says, "to be saved means to be rescued, to be delivered from." Let's say you are walking across the street and from your blind side there's an onrushing car. At the last second someone knocks you aside so the car barely misses you. It could be said that you were being saved, rescued or delivered from being hit.

Likewise, if you were out swimming and about to drown, and someone grabbed you before you went down for the last time, it could be said that you were saved from drowning. You were delivered. You were rescued.

The Bible teaches that every man born into the human race needs a form of rescuing, some kind of saving. I can almost hear many of you react to that one . . . I can hear you say, "You Christians are all alike. You're going to say I need to be saved from hell and the lakes of brimstone and fire. I need to be 'delivered out of the pit.' You're trying to *scare* me into the kingdom of God. All you preachers are alike! You just play on people's emotions and fears."

That is *not* what I am going to tell you. I am not going to describe a devil with a pitchfork in his hand, a funny sneer on his face, and a long pointed tail. But I am telling you that *you do need to be saved.* And do you know what you need to be saved from? The Bible teaches that you need to be saved from *yourself! You* are your own biggest problem.

The Bible says that every person born into the human race is born without the life of God. He is born independent of that life. It is the absence of God's life in a man that makes a man a sinner.

A man is not a sinner because he lies.
A man is not a sinner because he steals.

A man is not a sinner because he commits adultery.

A man is not a sinner because he commits murder. Those sins are a *result* of his sinful nature. A man sins because he is a sinner. Any person who does not have God's life in him is a sinner. You could be the most respectable person in the community; you could go to church every Sunday; you could give most of your money to religious causes; you could be a good neighbor — but the Bible teaches that if you do not have the life of God in you, you are a sinner.

The Bible also says that *all* have sinned and come short of the glory, or standards, of God. You see, God doesn't go around comparing people, He thinks in terms of their lives. All men are equal in His sight.

Therefore, when we mention sin, we're not talking just about the corrupt acts. We are not talking about the sinful things people do. Rather, we are talking about man's nature.

Every person is born biologically alive, but the Bible teaches that he is born spiritually dead. Every person born into the human race is born without the life of God. *That* is what makes men sinners. Long before that baby does anything wrong, the Bible says he is a sinner. Not because he does bad things but because he is born without the life of God.

So when the Bible says that man needs to be saved, it teaches that he needs to be saved from *himself*. Man is thoroughly corrupt. The Bible cuts across the old concept that, "All of us have some good in us and it is just a matter of going around and fanning this little divine spark until it bursts into glorious flame." The Bible rejects this philosophy totally.

There was a young man who came to Jesus one night and he addressed Him, "Good master," and Jesus immediately reprimanded him.

"Why do you call Me good? There is none good but God." Of course, Jesus was saying, in essence, "If you are prepared to call Me good, then you should be prepared to call Me God. Because there is none good but God."

If God is the only standard of good, then *man can't be good* unless he has God in him. Because God is the only standard of good, when we talk about righteousness, when we talk about morality, we are talking about God — about the life of God in a man. Remember, the Bible teaches that everyone born into the human race is born without the life of God. And because man does not have God's life in him, he is not capable of reproducing the standards established by a holy God. He is not capable of living up to the rules of God. He cannot keep *one,* let alone all of the Ten Commandments. He is not capable of living up to the Sermon on the Mount or of obeying the Golden Rule.

A man once asked me, "Mr. Skinner, wouldn't you agree that people would be basically good as long as they treated their neighbors as themselves and obeyed the Golden Rule?" I told him I agreed with that, but the problem is *there isn't one person in the world who has the ability to obey the Golden Rule.* Man doesn't have the power to be what God wants, because he doesn't have God in him. The apostle Paul put it essentially this way, in the seventh chapter of Romans: "I know that in me — that is, in my self-life — there dwells no good thing." In other words he said, "I've come to the conclusion that I'm a corrupt man. The will to do good is present with me. In my mind I want to serve God; in my mind I want to do the will of God, to live up to all the standards of God. But I just can't seem to perform that which is good. I find myself doing that which I *don't* want to. Instead, I find that when I would do good, evil is present with me."

Have you ever had that experience? Have you ever had the experience of going to bed at night and looking back over the day, sorry about some of the things you did or said? And maybe you decided, "Tomorrow morning things will be different." But you know when you "turn over a new leaf" you soon find yourself right back in the same rut.

Have you ever made New Year's resolutions? How many did you keep past January 2? You see, you just don't have the power to do it. A man without God can't measure up to his own standards, let alone the standards of God. We just can't live up even to our own expectations. Like Paul, we *want* to do good, but find ourselves doing evil instead.

There is another illustration. America, on paper, has the greatest Constitution in the world. When you sit down and read the Constitution of the United States you would almost think it was describing heaven. The big problem is that what we have on paper, and the ability of the American people to live up to those principles, are two different things. Although we in America are committed to democracy, we don't have the power to be democratic. That's our problem. Paul says, "When I want to do good, evil is present with me."

Or, let's take another example. Every year thousands of couples march down the aisle, stand before a priest, minister, justice of the peace, or rabbi and vow to stay together "until death do us part." Yet, we are told two out of every three marriages in American society ends up in the divorce court. Those people who stood before the altar were sincere, loved each other, and really wanted to spend their lives with each other. But they didn't have the power to pull it off. They didn't have the ability to carry out their vow.

You see, man is helpless; he is powerless, because of his corrupt nature — the result of his independence from God. He doesn't have the ability to keep those promises.

So Paul is saying about his dilemma, "I am powerless to do good. Who will rescue me? Who will save me?"

That's man's problem. Who will rescue me from this sinful nature that infests my own life? Who will deliver me from my spiritual death and bondage to sin?

Paul says in Romans 7:25 that Jesus Christ is the person

who delivers from spiritual death. How? Very simple. Jesus
Christ was the only man who had the ability to live up to all
God's demands. He was the only one able to live without
sinning, without falling short of God's standards, because He
was God's Son. He was with God before the foundations of
the world; He was the Lord from heaven. And the Bible says
He was worthy to bear the independent sinful nature with
which you and I are born. He assumed our place, our role,
in receiving punishment for sins. Because we are sinners, the
Bible says Jesus was nailed to the cross. He did it for you,
and for me . . . He willingly died so we might live. That's why
Scripture says He, Jesus Christ, who knew no sin, *became* sin
that we, through Him, might become the righteousness of
God.

Let me explain that.

Jesus Christ, realizing that death was close, went into a
garden called Gethsemane and prayed. In essence, He said
to His Heavenly Father, "If it is possible for this bitter cup
to pass, let it be. Nevertheless, not My will but Your will be
done." What was the bitter cup? Was Jesus Christ afraid of
death? Absolutely not. Then why was He saying "let this
bitter cup pass from me"? It seemed almost as if He wanted
to back out. No, Christ was not afraid of death. It was not
the physical suffering He feared. Remember, men took Jesus,
whipped Him, beat Him, crushed a crown of thorns over His
head. They put a heavy cross on His shoulders and forced
Him to carry it to Calvary. Then He endured the agony of
being nailed to the cross. It has been said that crucifixion is
the most horrible, cruel and physically painful form of killing a man. But Jesus endured it all. He was no coward. He
willingly took everything they dished out — and cried out
only to forgive His tormentors. No . . . He was no coward.
That was suffering; that was pain. But that is not what He
feared.

The fear, the agony, that Jesus faced when He hung on

that cross came when His Heavenly Father turned His back on Him. When Christ hung on that cross, He was left alone.

Why did His Father leave Him alone? Because a holy, righteous God cannot even look upon sin. When God the Father looked down on that cross, He did not see the Son with whom He shared eternity, long before the foundations of the world. On that cross He saw *you and me,* in all of our filth, independence, alienation, and sin. And God had to turn His back. He could not look upon sin and He had to leave His Son, the Lord Jesus Christ, hanging there by Himself, suffering in our place, experiencing the agony and hell we deserve. He did this *for us.* That was the "bitter cup." That is what Jesus dreaded.

The Bible declares that Christ took our sinful, rotten human natures with Him to the cross and put them to death. Someone has rightly said that He "killed death dead." Remember, we are born spiritually dead; He took that dead nature with which we are born and crucified it. That is why He cried on the cross, "It is finished," or in essence, "I have put to death, once and for all, the rotten human nature of humanity."

The Bible declares that on that cross He did something else. And this is important. He shed His blood to forgive us every sin we have ever committed as a result of our independence and alienation from God. The Bible declares that three days after Christ's death, Jesus Christ rose up from the grave, merely to prove He had power over death. He got up out of the grave so that He could offer His resurrected life to any person who wanted to "come alive." Jesus Christ is the only person with real life in the universe. He said, "I have come that they might have life and that they might have it more abundantly." That is why the apostle John records Jesus saying in essence, "I am the way, the truth and the life. There is no way by which you can begin to experience spiritual life with the energy of God in you until you come to Me."

That is what the Bible is saying when it says *He is able to save*. Whenever you are biologically, intellectually and nervously alive, you have made the first step toward becoming spiritually alive. For Jesus Christ has offered this new life to all who will receive Him. The Bible warns that "the wages of sin" — willful independence from God, turning your back on the life, freedom and forgiveness He offers — will result in your continuing to be spiritually dead. You will spend eternity in this dead state, separated from God forever. The Bible calls this separation *hell*. But Christ will impregnate your humanity so that God's life will flow into your life.

That's what it means to be saved. When you take a long look at your life, admit you're a sinner, independent, and doing your own thing, running your own life — then you have recognized you are spiritually dead and need to be saved from this condition and its ultimate consequences. When you get to that point, sorry for your past and sinful separation from God — the moment you ask Jesus Christ to come in and live in you, to flood your humanity with Himself and His power — that is when you are saved. That is the moment when you are delivered from yourself — rescued from yourself.

The Bible describes this new life in John 3:36, "He that believeth on the son hath everlasting life." And no one can ever take this new life away from you. Once you have it, you can't lose it. That's what it means to be saved. It's a simple matter.

You say, "Yeah, but Tom, suppose I *do* that thing? Suppose I commit myself to Jesus Christ, give my life to Him. You don't know me, man. You don't know how weak I am. I have problems. I have to go back to my neighborhood, my house, my school, my job, all kinds of things. I have to go back and face all these temptations and problems. I'm afraid if I commit my life to Jesus Christ, I'll go back out there and fall in the same trap. I mean, I'm so overwhelmed by temptation — I just can't live the kind of life you're describing.

What can your God do in that area?"

The apostle Paul, anticipating your question, says this: "I know in whom I have believed, and am persuaded that *he is able to keep that which I've committed unto him* against that day." *He is able to keep.* You see, Jesus Christ doesn't come into your life and then "cop out" on you. It's not a matter of meeting some sort of crisis, then you ask Christ into your life, and then you have to go out and break your neck to be a Christian in the middle of the same old temptations. You see, God already knows you *can't* be a Christian. God already knows it's impossible for you to live up to the Christian standard. If you could be a Christian in your own strength, there would be no need for Jesus Christ.

But in essence the apostle Paul is saying, "Once you commit your life to Jesus Christ, He saves you from yourself — your sinful nature — and He forgives you every sin you've ever committed." Whatever sin you may have committed in the past, God has completely wiped it out the moment you come to Him. That means you don't ever have to feel guilty about anything you've done in the past once you commit yourself to Jesus Christ. Once Jesus Christ comes into your life, there's no need for you to have nightmares or feel guilty about something you've done. The Bible essentially declares: "The blood of Jesus Christ, God's son, cleanses you *from every sin.*" You stand in the presence of God as if you had *never* sinned.

But Jesus does more than that. Not only does He save you and forgive you, *He keeps you.*

I once heard a person say, "You know, when you become a Christian, it's like you're hanging onto a rope and you have to hold on to that rope real tight, because underneath is the pit of hell and if you let go, you're going to fall right in."

That's a lot of nonsense. That is not what the Bible teaches. *The Christian life is not you holding on to God. The Christian life is God holding on to you.*

And there's a vast difference! That's why the Bible says when a person commits himself to Jesus Christ, *underneath* are the everlasting arms; *underneath* is God upholding you. Jesus says to the person who comes to Him, "I will never leave you nor forsake you, for I am with you always — even unto the end of the age." And listen to what He says in John 10:28 to those who come to Him: "I've given to them eternal life and they shall never perish." What does the word "eternal" mean? It means forever. What does the word "never" mean? It means it can't happen. What He means is, "I give unto them life forever and they shall never (it cannot happen) perish, neither shall any man pluck them out of My hand."

My friend, it's as simple as this: I have the life of Jesus Christ in me forever and no one can take me out of the hand of God. I am secure in Him.

You say, "But wait a minute, Tom. What you say sounds as if it gives a person license to do whatever he wants. I mean, if you have everlasting life and will never perish, then you can go out and do whatever you want. You can go out and commit all kinds of sin because God has given you eternal life and won't take it away."

If you think this, my friend, you misunderstand. You don't come to Jesus Christ for the purpose of *stopping* certain things. This is where we're all messed up. We think people need Jesus Christ because they do bad things. That is not why people need Jesus Christ. It is not because they do evil things. A man needs Jesus Christ because he is born without the life of God. You don't need Jesus Christ because you're a drunkard. You don't need Jesus Christ because you take drugs. You don't need Jesus Christ because you lie. You don't need Jesus Christ because you cheat on your income tax. No, you don't need Jesus Christ because you do bad things. That's not why you need Christ. Whether you've done any of those things is irrelevant. *You need Jesus Christ because you're born without the life of God.* That makes you a sinner. You don't have God's life in you. The Bible declares God has come to put His life in you and once His life is in you, it will never be taken away. And once Christ comes in you, He brings power and supernatural love. He puts the love of God in you. And out of your love for Him you *want* to do His will. No one who loves God deliberately wants to back out when it comes to serving Him.

It also means when you commit yourself to Jesus Christ *you don't have any more problems*. I know that grabs you. I had better break that down for you. Let me illustrate it this way.

If you own a home and the roof caves in, who has to have it repaired and foot the bill? You do. It's your home. But let's say I sat down and negotiated to buy your house, and we had all the lawyers and everyone present to take care of the whole thing, so that you passed title of your house to me today. So, if the roof caved in tomorrow morning, whose problem would it be? Mine, not yours any more, because you passed title of that home on to me.

The apostle Paul is saying, "There was a moment when I ran my own life and when problems developed, they were my problems. I had to sweat them out. But there came a moment in my life when I trusted Jesus Christ. And because I trusted Him, I've given Him my life. I 'passed title' of my life to Jesus Christ. Now my life belongs to Him, so any problem that develops in this 'property' is not my problem. It's God's problem because He has title to my life."

Now let me clarify that so you don't get the idea that the problems in your life automatically go away. No, problems don't disappear. Your problems will still be there. In fact, if you commit your life to Jesus Christ, you will probably have more problems in the next forty-eight hours than you've had in the last forty-eight days. No, I'm not telling you that your problems will *disappear*; I'm telling you that they will no longer be *your* problems — they will be *His*. Jesus Christ doesn't come to *remove* your problems, He comes to give you the strength to learn how to give your problems to Him. He gives you the direction, purpose and power you need to solve your problems. That's what it is all about.

That's why the Bible teaches the Christian to "cast your burdens upon the Lord, for He careth for you." If you cast all your burdens upon Him, how many burdens do you have left? None. If you cast everything on Him, it is then Christ's problem. He deals with your concerns and troubles. It would seem better to let Him do the sweating, to let Christ solve your problem. He's in a better position to do so. He is able to deal with them — because the Bible tells us He has gone through the same temptations but without sin.

Finally, we read in Jude 24, "Now unto him who is *able to keep you from falling* and to present you faultless before his (God's) presence in glory with exceeding joy." "Unto him who is able to keep you from falling" — what do we mean by falling — does that mean that you won't make any mistakes when you become a Christian? No. Does it mean that you won't commit any sin if you become a Christian? No. That's not what it means.

The difference between a sinner and a Christian is this. A person who doesn't know Christ practices sin. He is a sinner by nature. It is natural for him to sin. A person who commits himself to Jesus Christ may commit sin, but *he no longer practices sin*. He is no longer a sinner by nature. He is no longer acting totally independent from God. That's the difference.

When the Bible says that Christ will keep you from falling, it means He will keep you from falling into a state where you completely depend upon yourself. He will keep you from falling back into a place where you run your own life, do your own thing, totally apart from God. He will *uphold* you, and keep you from falling into the tragic eternal consequences of being a sinner.

A person who commits himself to Jesus Christ no longer has to worry about the judgment of God. God has delivered him "against that day," the day of judgment, when the books shall be opened and men are judged. Jesus Christ liberates him from the fear of judgment and keeps him from falling.

Jesus Christ will present you to God on that day of judgment as faultless, without spot, without blemish, in the presence of His own glory. To me that's exciting — especially when I reflect on how bigoted, how evil, how violent, how prejudiced my past has been.

I had reached the place where I had no conscience. I could break a bottle across a fellow's head, take the broken, jagged half, and twist it into his face without batting an eye. My knife blade went into twenty-two different guys and I never flinched. I had no sense of mercy or conscience.

But all that is past — completely erased because I have committed myself to a Christ who lived, died in my place, and rose again. Because of that, He has radically changed me, forgiven me of every sin I've ever committed. I no longer have to feel guilty about my past. And one day in the future, He's going to take me in spite of my inadequacy, in spite of my weakness, and will present me to God as if I were dressed in His own righteousness and glory. That turns me on! And that's what He's talking about. *He has that ability.*

There is no one else in all the universe who has the ability to do that. You can talk about changing the world all you want. You cannot change the world until you come to a realization that you, *yourself,* are messed up . . . until you see that Christ died for messed up people and rose from the dead to give them new life. Christ is the only person who changes individuals, the first step in changing the world.

God is working on the earth to attract people to Himself. No matter what revolutions take place, God has a revolution of His own going on. And He is saying, "It's *My* revolution that really counts."

To summarize, the Bible says that Jesus Christ is able. He is able to save you from yourself. He is able to keep you from falling back into the old way of life. He is able to do "exceedingly abundantly above all that you can ask or think." He is able to rescue you out of temptation. He is able to keep you safe in the day of judgment. That is what Jesus is offering to you now. He asks, "Do you want Me, do you want My life? Do you want to trust Me, do you want to commit yourself to My ability?"

Notice that among all the Bible verses listed in this chapter, not one says *you* are able? The fact of the matter is *you* are *not* able.

You do not have the ability to be what God wants.

Remember, you don't have the ability to live up to your own standards, let alone God's. God says that if you go out in your own strength and ability to reproduce the Christian life you will fall flat on your face. It is impossible. You need God to make it possible for you to be a Christian; it takes God even to be a man in the fullest sense. You don't become a real man or woman until your life has been impregnated with the life of God.

Are you willing to trust that Christ? Because, you see, no matter how much I tell you about Jesus — about His ability, uniqueness, sufficiency and adequacy to do His thing in you — it's all worthless until you come to trust Him. So, I'm inviting you to come to Jesus Christ.

God wants you to become the vehicle through which He expresses Himself. That's what "having faith" means. Having faith means letting Jesus Christ come inside and live in you.

Do you want that?

Do you really want to "come alive"?

Then ask Jesus Christ to come to you with His free gift of forgiveness and new life, recognizing that He alone has the unique *ability* to do all these wonderful things He has promised to do.

7

By Whose Authority?

We are living in a very sick society.

And those of us under the age of thirty find it especially difficult to cope with the frustrations and problems of men. We have been offered many solutions in the short time we have lived, only to see most of them explode in our faces.

Many of us, as idealistic young people, committed ourselves to try to change the system. Many of us chose idealistic leaders who had charisma and philosophical idealism. We admired their courage as they dared to stand up and challenge the world and the systems of men. Many of them even challenged the immorality and injustice of our times. But in the last six years, we young people have seen our idealistic leaders shot down before our eyes. Whether men of great charisma like John or Robert Kennedy . . . men who had great social prophetic vision, like Martin Luther King, who spoke with great moral conscience to our nation . . . or whether it was that young tough-minded philosophical prophet known as Malcolm X . . . or men in the fields like Medgar Evers, we saw idealistic leaders. These were men of courageous thoughts and great sensitivity to social issues, men who seem to have come along in history at the right time. Yet, we saw them shot down before our very eyes.

These tragedies have disillusioned many of our young people who now feel there is no hope, no way we can possibly change the system.

The prevailing mood of complete hopelessness has caused many middle and upper-class young people to "cop out" on society. Still others have chosen to "trip out" on drugs to get away from it all. They want to escape because they don't have the power to deal with a frustrated world.

Yes, there is absolutely no doubt in our minds that society is deteriorating. There is no doubt that we live in an immoral time in the history of our country and in the history of men.

It isn't a problem of being able to diagnose the situation. Most of us can tell what the problems are. Many of us can even offer sensible solutions. But the issue is not figuring out what the problems are, but coming up with men and women who have the power, the ability and the authority to do something about them.

Plato wrote an exciting description of what he considered a utopian society and what has become known classically as a Plato republic. He built his dream world where humanity would be ruled by great men of superb philosophical intelligence, men who had been disciplined into a tough-mindedness from their youth through maturity. These men would have studied all the great sciences, disciplines and philosophies until they were intellectually and mentally capable of ruling the world. But when he had finished building this dream world, Plato closed it by saying, "Alas, I have built a perfect republic but I have *no perfect men* to rule my perfect republic."

That is the issue: How do you bridge the gap between what we are idealistically committed to and what we can pragmatically execute? How do we bridge the gap between our theory and our ability?

Richard Nixon, while whistle-stopping through a midwestern town during his last campaign, pledged to the American people to "bring America together again." He has discovered, of course, since taking office that it is not as easy as he thought it would be. America is far more fragmented and more divided than ever before and tensions are still running high. There is as great a polarization as ever and people still haven't learned how to live and work together.

Numbers of people are "copping out" on the society because they feel they have no reason to live. So in the middle of all of this, the issue is still, "Where do we get the power and authority to do what we know ought to be done?"

We know we live in a society of racism, but where do we get the power to end racism?

We know we live in a society where there is injustice, but where do we get the power to end injustice?

We know large numbers of people go to bed hungry every night, but where do we get the power to feed them?

We know if we continue to pollute our air and water, life on earth will soon be impossible — but where do we get the power to stop the trend?

We know all of that, but the question is *how do we stop these trends?* Where do we get the power to bring about a noble society? — a democratic society? Where do we get the power to teach people how to live, to relate, "to love mercy, to do justice and walk humbly before their God"? It is not a question of knowing what is right and wrong — the issue is how do we take action in light of our knowledge?

You will recall it was the apostle Paul, writing in the seventh chapter of Romans, who said in essence, "In my mind, I want to serve God, in my mind I want to do the will of God, in my mind I want to do what is right, somehow I can't seem to perform that which is good, and that which I *don't* want to do, I end up doing. I want to do good, but end up doing wrong instead. What's wrong with me?" You see,

Paul knew he didn't have the power to do good, even though he desperately wanted to do so.

But Paul wasn't unique. The same is true of all men through history. When I read about great men who walked the face of the earth, I become even more frustrated because I discover *no men in history had the power to be what they ought to be.*

But then, I come into contact with this very contemporary, radical person, known in history as Jesus Christ. I encountered a man who has authority, who's learned how it really is. Not only is He tough-minded, intelligent and disciplined, not only does He know right from wrong, but He has the authority and the power to go out and do what is right.

I was turned on by Jesus Christ. I wanted to discover the secret of His life, to know why He was different from any other man who walked the face of the earth. I did learn something of the secret of His life, but I don't want to give you the wrong impression of Jesus Christ because of what He has done for me. Rather, I want you to check out Jesus Christ for yourself.

I was in a search for someone in the world, perhaps in history, who was different from any other man who ever lived. I studied Alexander, Napoleon and other great leaders from the past. My whole search was for a radical, contemporary, yet compassionate individual who was plugged into both God and man. I wanted someone who could be a living model of what man ought to be. My search was for someone who could smash injustice, smash racism, smash oppression. I wanted someone who could deal mercifully and fairly with the issues and the problems of our time. And in all of history I could not discover a man who was committed both to the spiritual laws of God and to the moral laws of humanity. I could not discover anyone who had great moral ideals and the power to administrate them — until I ran into this individual, Jesus Christ. He was the only person who seemed to possess the power and authority to be what man ought to be.

In the seventh chapter of Luke I read about a very interesting facet of His power. In essence the story is as follows: "When He ended teaching the people, He went to a place called Capernaum. And a certain Centurion had a servant who was very close to him. His servant was sick and ready to die. When he heard of Jesus, he sent unto Him the leaders of the Jews, begging Him that He should come and heal the servant. And when they came to Jesus, they begged Him saying that this Centurion was worthy 'because he loves our nation and has built us a synagogue.' Jesus went with them and when He was not far from the house, the commander of soldiers sent his friends to Jesus, saying to Him, 'Lord, don't trouble Yourself. I am not worthy that You should enter my house, neither do I consider myself worthy to come out and talk to You, but just say the word and my servant will be healed, for I also am a man under authority. For I have under me soldiers, and I say unto one go and he goes, and I say unto another come and he comes, I say unto another one, do this and he does it.' When Jesus heard these things, He was amazed. He turned about and said to the people that followed Him, 'I have not found faith like this in all of Israel.' "

Now what was it about the man's statement that turned Jesus on? Here was a Centurion (which meant that he was the commander of 100 soldiers) who was part of the Roman system. Jews did not like Romans because they were exploiting Israel. But these elders of the Jews came to Jesus and said, "This Roman is not like other Romans. He loves our nation, he has built us a synagogue. He has dealt justly with us, he's not like the other Romans that run around our neighborhood. You should do this for him."

When Jesus drew near the man's house, the Centurion sent his friends out to Jesus and said, "Look, don't trouble Yourself to come to my house, because I'm not worthy." Keep in mind that this is a Roman talking to a Jew. Very seldom did Romans tell Jews they weren't worthy of *anything* in connection with a Jew! A Roman told a Jew whatever he wanted to and the Jew had to respond. But here was a Roman who saw beyond Jesus simply being a Jew; he saw something else. And he said, "Just say the word and my servant will be healed. I also am a man under authority."

Now that was the secret. "I also am a man under authority." And we read that Jesus was surprised. Now what was so profound about that statement that Jesus got all excited about it? Very simple, the secret is wrapped up in the words, "I also am a man under authority." The Centurion is saying that anyone who wants power, anyone who wants authority has to be under someone else's authority to get it.

If you have a private in the United States Army, somewhere around there's a corporal; if you find a corporal, there's a sergeant. A sergeant can't have authority or power unless there's someone with more rank, so you will find a lieutenant, or a captain. Wherever there is a captain, there is someone who gave him the authority, so you run into a major, colonel or a general. And even the general has been given his power and authority by someone. In other words, every man who has power has to be *under authority* to have that power.

Here was a man who said to Jesus, "I also am a man under authority." He recognized that Jesus also had authority. He said, "I've heard about Your power — how You've told dead people to come alive and they did. I've heard that You've given sight to blind people who have never seen in their lives. I've been told You have healed people who can't hear, people who haven't walked from birth are walking. No one can tell dead people to get up out of the grave; no one can tell blind people to see; no one can tell deaf people to hear; no one can tell lame people to walk, unless he has *power,* unless he has *authority.*"

The Centurion recognized the principle of authority and

said, in effect, "Lord, it's not necessary for You even to come to my house — I don't have the kind of power You do — so, I'm certainly not worthy to receive You. But I know that no one can do these works that You have done without a power that transcends all human power. Therefore, just say the word, Lord, and I'll know my servant will be healed."

That's why Jesus was amazed — He saw in the Centurion a faith greater than any He had seen, even in Israel.

Remember, Jesus never really performed any miracles. It was His Heavenly Father who sent Him from heaven who performed these things. Jesus in essence expressed it this way, "That which I do, My Father does it in Me" and, "I do only those things which please My Father" and again, "I have not come to do My will."

Keep in mind that Jesus Christ has a will of His own. He could have easily done His own will. But Jesus set aside His will to bring Himself under subjection to the will of His Father. Every move Jesus made, His Father made in Him. Every word He spoke, His Father who sent Him spoke through Him. Every deed He performed, His Father performed through Him. That's where Jesus Christ got His authority. He never once made a move without His Father. That's why He said to His disciples, "Don't believe Me simply because you see Me performing miracles. I want you to believe Me because the works that I do, My Father is doing in Me." Jesus Christ asked people to accept His credibility not by what He did, but by virtue of what His Heavenly Father did through Him.

I've said it before, but it bears repeating — what made Jesus Christ the most unique man in all of history was that He never once made a move on His own. He never did anything on His own. He lived totally under the authority of the Father who sent Him. And it was because He was constantly dependent upon His Father that He was perfect. If you'll check out the temptation of Jesus Christ in the wilderness, you will notice that He was never asked by Satan to do anything really absurd. He wasn't asked to get drunk, commit adultery, steal, lie or kill. Satan simply said, "If You are the Son of God, command that these stones be turned into bread."

Now ask yourself, what in the world is sinful about making bread out of stones?

Absolutely nothing.

Then why would Satan tempt Jesus with a simple thing like making bread out of stone? Simple. It was really a cunning trap. He was really trying to get Jesus to perform an act of power, acting on His own without consulting God the Father. And if He could have trapped Jesus into acting independently of His Father *just once,* He would have had Christ pegged as a sinner like anyone else.

Satan tried to get Jesus to do His own thing, apart from His Father, but it failed. Christ sent the devil away.

Jesus Christ lived under the absolute authority of His Father and that is why there was nothing He did without His Father. That is what made Him unique. That is what made Him who He was, what gave Him *His* authority and power. And because He committed Himself to His Father, His Father committed Himself to Jesus. So, in essence Christ was saying, "Because I am under the will of My Father and available to Him, He is available to Me. His *power* is available to Me. I can tell sick people to come alive. I can take bread and feed thousands of people because His power is available to Me."

Now, look at the implications of that for you and me. In essence Jesus says in the sixth chapter of John, "As I live, or depend upon My Father, so whoever depends upon Me shall live by Me. I derive My life and power from My Father. All My spiritual energy, discipline, morality and goodness come from My Father. Whoever makes himself available to Me, the way I'm available to My Father, then I will be available to him, the way My Father is available to Me. So that whatever My Father can do in Me, I will do in you."

Was it true? Would Jesus give this power to others as His Father had given it to Him? Let's find out from an illustration in the third chapter of Acts. Peter and John were going around Jerusalem preaching an explosive message about a radical Christ who was crucified. Remember, the Romans and Jewish authorities thought they had gotten rid of Him, but Jesus had burst out of the grave, *alive*. This radical message hit the streets of Jerusalem and had begun to turn the whole Roman Empire upside down.

One afternoon Peter and John were on their way to the temple to pray. Sitting at the gate of the temple was a man whom the Bible says was lame from his mother's womb. He had never walked in his entire life. The man sat at the gate of the temple holding out his hands to beg money from people as they came by. People would walk by, drop gold or silver coins in his hand or cup, and go on up to the temple to pray.

These wonderfully religious people would drop in a coin and forget any further obligation to the poor man. Once inside the temple, they would thank God that they weren't lame, making loud noises also about their own piety, congratulating themselves for "holding on to biblical truth while the liberalists and modernists were contaminating the Word of God." When it was all over — the benediction given and the doxology sung — they marched back down the steps of the temple right past that lame man, leaving him there.

Of course, in their pious pilgrimages back and forth, they must have passed him dozens — perhaps hundreds — of times. But all they ever did was to drop a few coins in his tin cup and say, "God bless you." No one ever made an attempt to deliver the man from his misery.

Oh, they tried to make him comfortable where he was. And unfortunately, that's what is happening in our society today. We're compassionate, so we try to make people more comfortable in their misery. But we do absolutely nothing to *deliver them* from their misery.

The same was true that day in Jerusalem. Only this time the beggar confronted Peter and John. He held out his hand to beg money of them. And you'll recall those classic words of Peter, "Silver and gold we don't have, but such as we *do* have, we give to you. In the name of Jesus Christ of Nazareth, rise up and walk!"

And the Bible tells us the man got up and walked. Now where did Peter and John receive their power for such an act? From Jesus Christ, of course. They said, "We tell you in His name to get up and walk." The man believed they had the power and authority to take care of his needs, so he got up and walked. That's what I mean by authority!

And this is what attracted me to Christ. My search ended when I met Him. Jesus had a kind of charisma, a kind of discipline, a kind of aura about Him that shook me.

I read in the Bible how the religious establishment in Jerusalem was up tight and jealous when it heard about Jesus. The people of this establishment decided He needed to be removed. He knocked their system; He was a threat to their religious establishment. They thought He was about to disrupt everything they had going if He had His way and the people followed Him. So they drummed up false charges against Him and sent the temple police to arrest Jesus.

When the police got to where Jesus was teaching and preaching, there was a crowd. So the police waited — and listened. When it was all over, they returned to headquarters without Him.

When they got back, the high priest asked, "Where is He? We sent you to arrest that man. Where is He, why haven't you brought Him back?"

Dumbfounded, the Roman "fuzz" stood there and said, "Never a man spoke like that man. He doesn't speak as one of the Scribes or Pharisees. He doesn't stand up there with a lot of double talk; He speaks as though He has authority."

This authority was evident when He was finally arrested and brought before Pilate. Pilate interrogated Him, playing a political game, but inwardly and morally wanting to let Christ go. Pilate turned to Jesus and said, "Look, don't You know that as Roman governor, I have the authority to release You, even though people out there are hollering for Your blood? Don't You know I have the authority to let You go?"

Then Jesus spoke up and said in today's terms, "No . . . no one has the authority unless it comes from above. And I'd like you to know that you don't really have any authority. If worst came to worst and I really needed to get out of this bag, I could call legions of angels right now. You don't have that kind of authority unless you're under authority."

That's the kind of Jesus I discovered — charismatic, disciplined, tough, radical — because He lived His life in total dependency upon His Father, not afraid to buck the establishment, the system, or to fight immorality and injustice. He was an individual.

And I'm saying if the world today is really going to be changed, it will be done only by people who are *under authority* — people, who by virtue of deriving their life from Jesus Christ, are totally dependent upon Him. They must be committed and can't be bought by any other system. And because they can't be bought, they can go out and address themselves prophetically, morally and ethically to the issues — without feeling intimidated. Why? Because they don't draw their authority from the system. They draw it from God who is Lord of heaven and earth. He is *above the system!*

Jesus Christ couldn't be bought. He wouldn't play the system's game. A classic example of this is found in the New Testament. It was Passover time, the great Jewish festival, in Jerusalem.

The austere rabbis, the great theologians, and all the respected Jewish teachers came to town for the occasion. The common people of Jerusalem had lined the roads to watch these great theologians, rabbis, and preachers come riding in.

One great rabbinical teacher came through in a Cadillac chariot. Another was driving a Continental — or its equivalent of that day. The people applauded when they recognized them.

"That is Rabbi So-and-so. He has written a great theological manuscript on whether forty-eight angels can sit on a pin!"

And there was similar applause for other respected teachers who came in, garbed in their best rabbinical finery.

Suddenly, there was a buzz through the crowd. People asked, "Who's that?"

Coming across the horizon was a different kind of man. He was not dressed in the great rabbinical robes and He was riding on the colt of an ass.

As He came nearer, a buzz went through the crowd, "Who's that?" "Who's He?"

Someone said, "I understand He's a simple street preacher, a carpenter from Nazareth, but marvelous things have been told us about Him. We've been told He can do miraculous things and that His teachings are profound. The word is He's knocking the whole Roman system. I hear He is smashing injustice and immorality wherever He finds it — whether in the temple or the streets. In His speaking to the system, He's a tough-minded man. There are some people who think He just might be the promised Messiah!"

And as the excitement about Jesus buzzed through the crowd, people began to tear down palm branches from the trees. They threw them in His path. They took their garments and spread them out as a carpet on the trail. They lifted up their voices in praise:

"Hosanna, Hosanna, blessed be the Son of David who cometh in the name of the Lord."

Shouts went up through the crowds to make Him king.

And as the crowd grew more excited, you could almost feel the tension, expecting Jesus to announce He was prepared to be King of Jerusalem. The crowd would have installed Him that day. He was at the height of His popularity.

And I can see His disciples looking at this great throng of people who are praising Him. They nudge each other and say, "Finally they've recognized our Lord. Finally they are giving Him the credit He deserves. Isn't it exciting? The whole town is in an uproar about Jesus. Man, He's finally going to be able to establish His kingdom. I just hope He doesn't say anything to botch it up."

I know how they felt. Jesus had a way of "botching things up" to their way of thinking. You know, if Jesus had had a press agent, He would have given the man fits. Every time Jesus was in the height of His popularity, He always did something to "lose votes" from the crowd. But then, because of His dependence upon His Father, He didn't need to play political games. Sure, He lost votes — He always separated the sincere from the insincere. When He finished a sermon or performed a miracle and great throngs of people came after Him, He would turn around to the crowd and say, "If any man would come after Me, let him deny himself, take up his cross and follow Me." At that the crowd would dwindle.

He'd go out and heal the sick or raise the dead. Great crowds of people then followed. But then He stood up and said, "If any man would come after Me and does not forsake all that he has, he cannot be My disciple." And for some reason, the crowd would dwindle.

Jesus would go out and feed five thousand people and the crowd would again get excited — until Jesus stood up to say, "If any man wants to be My disciple and does not love Me above mother, father, sister, brother, husband, wife and his own life also, he cannot be My disciple." And the crowd would dwindle.

One day the crowd had dwindled because Jesus laid some

heavy things on their minds so there was no one left but His own disciples. And He said, "Don't you want to go, too?"

Peter replied, "Where shall we go? To whom shall we go? Only You have the words of everlasting life. You're the only man with authority. Where would we go?"

But as Jesus rides into Jerusalem, I can see Peter and the other disciples — hoping Jesus wouldn't open His mouth. "If we can just keep Him from saying anything until they install Him as king. If we can just keep the reporters away and keep Him from talking, we've got it aced."

But when they get to Jerusalem, sure enough, Jesus blows the whole thing.

He discovered they had desecrated the house of God by turning it into a den of commercialism. He walked in with whips, infuriated that the dignity and honor of God's house had been desecrated, and knocked over the money changers, driving the sacrificial animals out. In a display of holy anger, He cleansed the temple.

And man, did that get the religious establishment up tight!

They came to Him and in essence demanded, "Who in the world do You think You are? What gives You the right to do what You did? Where do You get the authority to go around knocking over tables and money changers?"

Jesus was very cool. He just stood there and replied simply, "My Father. It is written that My Father's house shall be a house of prayer, but you've made it a den of thieves." That was just what they wanted to hear! You see, Jesus Christ was committed to morality; He was committed to justice. He was committed to the things that count. The religious establishment was up tight because He went out and rubbed shoulders with prostitutes and drunkards. He was often seen with people that society, even the religious society, had turned their backs on. And as they questioned Him about it, again He would fall back on His authority: "I have been sent by My Father. I have come to minister to those who need Me.

Those who are whole don't need a physician. I've come to
seek and to save that which was lost." He wasn't afraid to
tell it like it was — to lay it on the line — because He didn't
have to play games with the politicians in town. He received
His power and His authority from His Father.

Now what I'm saying by all this is that you can talk all you
want about revolution, you can talk all you want about going
out and smashing the establishment, but you have to keep in
mind that the establishment, the systems of men, are based
and rooted in power. If you think you are going to smash
the corrupt system, you're mistaken. The trouble is — you
also have a corrupt nature. The only way you are going to
smash the corrupt system is with a sense of justice, a sense
of power, a sense of *divine energy.* We will never change the
system unless we start to have movements in America which
are not simply inspired by rhetoric, by people with charisma,
fine-sounding programs, and a good rap. We need a movement in America which is inspired of God, with His ap-
proval, and His authority.

No one is more committed to the urgency of civil rights
in America than I am. But any civil rights movement not
undergirded by a good biblical basis and perspective will fail.
If the movement is not structured on the Word of God, no
matter how just the cause, it will not stand.

No one is more committed than I am in seeking to bring
America to its knees. I am sick of the immorality, the hypocrisy and mythology of the "great American dream." And
no one is more committed to making America what it ought
to be than I am. But I am also smart enough to know there
cannot be a movement that smashes evil, sin and injustice
which is not structured on the Word of God, because only
God is qualified to deal with us in this way and only God can
ultimately pronounce judgment on systems, because you are
dealing with more than just a system. You are dealing with
a system that has power behind it. The Bible says the prince

of this world, Satan, has control of the world. The system lies in His hands. You see you're dealing with more than just evil administrations; you're dealing with more than just evil political parties. You're dealing with more than oppressive, evil governors, senators, mayors and business establishments. Behind all the evil is Satan, God's adversary. The system lies in the hands of a powerful being. You're not going to smash that system on your own. It takes God to deal with that.

So you can't talk about going out and changing the world unless you are under God's authority. The power of the universe and the authority granted by the One who created it are at your disposal.

If you are really interested in changing the world, you can only do it through Christ and the authority which He will share with you. If you are interested in changing people and delivering them from the oppressing system . . . if you're really interested in feeding the poor, the hungry and putting clothes on the naked . . . if you're interested in setting captive people free . . . if you're really interested in giving sight to the blind and healing to the sick — you can only do it within the authority of Jesus Christ. It becomes a workable power as you allow yourself to be impregnated with His life.

Where do you get your authority? They asked Jesus by what authority He did His various deeds and He responded by telling them His authority was given to Him by His Heavenly Father. Where do you get your authority? From the same source.

Has Jesus Christ come to live in you? Is Jesus Christ alive in you? I'm not talking about religion; don't tell me how religious you are; don't tell me what church you go to. I'm asking, "Is Jesus Christ living in you, do you get your authority from Him?"

He is the source of power and authority for changing the world.

And I'd like especially to challenge those who represent

the "now generation" . . . those of us who are in the "under-30" crowd, those who want to see the system changed.

Allow me to remind you that because we've done a better job in diagnosing how sick the world is, that doesn't make us any more moral than our parents. We have had the perception because of our youth, background, and education, to see things that our parents perhaps haven't been able to see. We've been able to see how messed up the system is. But we are not any more moral, we don't have more *power* than they have.

If you want to change the system of the world; if you want to see justice, mercy, and tranquility done; if you want to see oppressed and captive people liberated, then you must do something your parents didn't do. You must somehow become more moral. And I say, by the authority of God's Word, you can only become more moral through God's power — His Spirit — and the authority of God. You must let Christ rule in your life.

Then you can go out and change the world. I call you to that kind of a Christ right now.

I say to you that this Christ is alive right now. He is prepared to live His life in you. And regardless of the revolutions going on in the world, God has a revolution of His own. He is getting that revolution accomplished through His Son, Jesus Christ. So if you're not plugged into Jesus Christ, you're nowhere. Do you want to get plugged into Him? Allow Him to be Lord of your life — to give you complete direction, because that's what makes a Christian radical — radical according to the Scriptural definition, with purpose. As a Christian, you will be living under the authority, the Lordship, the ownership of Jesus Christ. And you can change the world!

Is this what you want? All you have to do is say, "Lord, I am prepared right now — with no strings attached — to give all that I am and all that I have totally to You. I even give You the right to run my life."

Remember, it has nothing to do with being religious, it has nothing to do with church at this point; it has to do with whether you want this Person, Jesus Christ, to run your life. If you do want Him to run your life, then I invite you to pray right now, "I want this power, I want authority. I'm willing to submit to authority to be a son of God. I want the authority to go out and live life the way God intended men to live. I want the authority that God gives in His name for those who want to work for good, to radicalize and change the system, the world."

If that is your desire, then turn to God. Ask His Son, the Lord Jesus Christ, to come into your life. There can be no justice, no liberation, no freedom until the great Liberator, Jesus Christ, is allowed to control your life and all your abilities. The amazing paradox of the Christian faith is that surrender to Christ's will means ultimate freedom. Turn to Him and turn on with His power and authority.

8

Revolutionary Power for Action

We have come to the point where we can ask ourselves — what does it take to bring about the kind of spiritual revolution needed to effectively change the system? Certainly such change can only be brought about by a spiritual awakening, or revival, in America.

But what is revival?

What does it mean to be Christian?

What does it mean to have spiritual awakening? Many people are confused about these terms and what they mean, so it might be well for us to define what we mean — and what we don't mean — by them.

When we talk about revival, what comes to mind? For some people, the word "revival" conjures up memories of what used to be called the "sawdust trail."

Many people think of revival as an emotional religious experience — some people getting happy and making noises about God. When I grew up and heard the word revival, it meant people jumping on the pews on Sunday morning.

And when some people think of the term "Christian," they think about people who go to church every Sunday at 11:00 o'clock, people who are actively engaged in church activity. Is that what a Christian is? For other people, a Christian is a person who is morally good. He treats his neighbors kindly and gets along with people; he's a good family man, makes an honest living, doesn't do anything really immoral. Is that what a Christian is?

And what about this term, "spiritual awakening"? Awakened from what? — to what?

For an answer I turn to the Bible, the only authority from which I can operate. I discover from the Scriptures something very significant about what it means to be Christian, about revival and spiritual awakening, and I would like to share it with you.

Our exploration begins in Acts 2:1. But, first allow me to fill you in on some of the background.

Jesus Christ came to earth and lived His life in total dependence upon His Father. The Bible says Jesus was the only man in all of history worthy to take on Himself our sinful, independent natures. He was crucified for us, died in our place, experienced the hell the whole human race deserved, to forgive us our sin. Then He rose from the dead to live His resurrected life in anyone who trusted Him. During the years of His public ministry, Jesus had gathered a group of disciples. They were men of differing political and economic views. There was Peter, a "fisherman." He got Peter to sit down with Him. He called Matthew, who was a tax collector, definitely a member of the establishment. And he got Matthew to sit down with Peter. He called out to John, by any standard an Uncle Tom. John's attitude was, "Don't rock the boat, baby. Leave it the way it is." But Jesus got John to sit down with Peter and Matthew. He called these men from different political hues. Some were militant, some were moderates, some were Uncle Toms, some were pacifists, some didn't care. And He got them to sit down with Him, to rap about a unique kind of revolution. He told them that God was out to bring about His own revolution, and that He, as the Son of God, had come to earth to do God's will and *start* God's revolution. But to do it, He needed men who would be committed to Him.

After His death and resurrection, Jesus spent about forty days with them, mapping out the strategy they were to use to go out and shake up a corrupt world. It was a new kind of message of liberation: *That men must first begin by being liberated from themselves, from their own independence and from their own alienation from God before they could go out and set other people free.*

Jesus told His disciples that before they could carry out this mission, they needed to have special power. They needed to have His power flooding their lives. So the book of Acts reminds us that Jesus told them to go to Jerusalem and wait until this power came. They came to Jerusalem. God told them to go to a particular room and wait until they received this power. They reached the room and looked around and noticed there were still only eleven disciples. You'll recall one had gone out and hanged himself. And they decided they needed to replace him. So they got together and took a vote.

It's interesting to note that God never told them to vote about anything, just to wait. But they decided to have an election. So they voted for another man whose name was Matthias. But it's also interesting to note how this man passes into obscurity. You never hear his name mentioned in the Bible again. Because, you see, apostles are not chosen by men. Apostles are chosen by God. One of the unfortunate things about religion in the twentieth century is that we have many religious leaders who have never really been chosen by God.

That is the background leading up to the second chapter of Acts. The Bible says that "when the actual day of Pentecost came, they were all assembled together as instructed. Suddenly there was a sound from heaven like the rushing of a violent wind, and it filled the house where they were seated. Before their eyes appeared what looked like tongues of flames, which separated and settled over the heads of each one of them. They were all filled with the Holy Spirit and began to speak different languages as the Spirit gave them power to proclaim His message" (Acts 2:1-4, Phillips).

The Bible says the Spirit of God came into the lives of these men in three forms. First, it came as wind; second, it came as fire; and third, it came as tongues.

The Spirit came as wind first. There was a sudden sound from heaven like a rushing, violent wind. Now, wherever you find wind mentioned in Scripture, you'll find it talking about regeneration. The word regeneration means to take that which is dead and make it alive. Wherever God is operating, you'll discover dead things — especially dead people — coming alive.

The Scripture teaches that every person born into the human race is born biologically alive, but spiritually dead. The Bible says, "The soul that sinneth it shall die." That means sin separates us from God. That accounts then for the reason the world is so messed up. It is because we are asking dead people to do living things. We walk up to a person who is spiritually dead and say: "Look, you're supposed to love everyone." Well, the Bible says a fruit of the Spirit, which is God's life, is love. Love is life. To ask a dead man to produce living fruit is asking the impossible. That man doesn't have the ability to love. We're saying to people who are dead, "Love your enemies. Be patient. Be kind. Have mercy. Do justice."

We're walking around waving the peace flag and saying, "Bring an end to war." And that's a noble commitment. I'm committed to bringing an end to war and bringing about peace and justice. But I also know that there is no way you can bring an end to war and have peace, justice, mercy, love, patience, temperance and goodness as long as you have dead people trying to do it.

No way!

You see, God wants to make people alive so they can do the "living" things He has called them to do. That's why the Bible teaches that wherever God is operating, there is life. God comes in and quickens the individual who trusts Him. So if you're talking about revival, if you're talking about being in the real Church, if you're talking about spiritual awakening, if you're talking about being a Christian — you're talking about an individual who was once dead but is now alive . . . who was once alienated from God but is now reconciled to God . . . who was once independent from God but is now dependent on God. That is the essence of what it means to be regenerated, to be made alive. There is no other way you can talk about revolution.

Now, I'm committed to revolution. Revolution is defined as taking an existing, unworkable, archaic or impractical situation and replacing it with a system that works. I'm committed to that. I'm convinced that the system is in a mess. Man's system has had God's judgment pronounced upon it. I'm convinced we live in an immoral time, an unjust time, a racist time, a militaristic time, and an oppressive time. I'm convinced of all that. But as long as you still have messed-up people, you'll never really solve the basic problem and your revolution is doomed before it starts.

So if you're talking about real revolution, you have to change both systems. And that's what the "wind" of God does. When God is at work, He is at work changing, regenerating, reviving that which has gone dead.

America is dead in the sense that she needs moral and spiritual awakening. Our systems and institutions are dead in the sense that God isn't operating through them. So if you're talking about a real revolution, you're talking about going out and offering a dead system new life. That life is found only in Jesus Christ.

The wind of God also speaks of revival — to take that which is fainting or in an unconscious state — and revive it.

The prophet Ezekiel stood up and looked across a vast valley of dry bones (which represented the nation of Israel, God's people who had now "gone dead" on God). The most they could do was sit around and eulogize themselves. They talked about their history, about the "good old days," about how God delivered them and brought plagues on Egypt. They reminisced about how God led them through the Red Sea and drowned the Egyptians, how God helped bring down the walls of Jericho with just a shout.

They eulogized their great past, yet their past was history. But you see, you don't eulogize *living* things. You eulogize that which is dead.

And the great problem we have today is that there are many people running around eulogizing America. "America, the beautiful. We must return to those great days of yesteryear when our country stood for freedom. We must go back to those days when we were a God-fearing nation."

They're always talking about going back. But when you talk about the past, you're eulogizing. You're pronouncing judgment. You don't eulogize something that's living. The very fact that we keep talking about what America *used to be* is indicative that something is wrong.

We are dead. And the eulogy is just part of the funeral service.

Unfortunately those of us in the church are doing the same thing. We're sitting down and talking about the good old days, the way it used to be.

Throughout history, God has expressed Himself. In essence He told people when they wanted to know who He was, "I Am. I am not yesterday, I am not tomorrow. I Am . . . today, *now,* present tense." I'm afraid some people make the same mistake of relegating God either to the past or to the future. They talk about the "Ebenezer, hitherto God has blessed us." Or they talk about the future. The Maranatha. "What God will do tomorrow."

One of the things that used to turn me off when I was a kid in church was people who were always standing up talking about the "good old days." They'd talk about "the revivals we used to have." They'd talk about the horse and buggy days when they walked for miles and miles to get out and hear the Word of God and see people really converted. I heard them tell how they would miss a whole meal to get out and hear the Word. And, they'd say, "we used to have great revivals fifty years ago."

Well, you know, my friend, I appreciate that. I appreciate *whenever* God has moved in history. I appreciate whatever God has done in the past. But my problem is, *I* wasn't around fifty years ago. I am twenty-eight years old. And I don't want to wait for tomorrow. *I want to know what is your God doing now, today, this hour!*

And so God was trying to bring Israel to a place where it stopped eulogizing itself . . . stopped talking about its history and its past . . . and started straightening itself out.

So there is this vast valley of dry bones, representing people who have gone dead on God. And God asks the prophet, "Can these dry bones live again?" And that is the question being asked in America today. "Can the church live again?"

"Can democracy live again?"

"Can brotherhood live again?"

And the prophet answers God, "Lord, only You know. Only you know." So the prophet stands up and cries out, "Come from the four winds, O breath, and breathe upon these slain that they may live."

Remember, this "wind" speaks of the ability of God to take that which is dead and make it alive. What we are saying here is if America is dead, if our institutions, churches or our educational systems, are not relevant and alive, it can only mean the life of God is not flowing through them.

We need God's Spirit to breathe on our "dead" nation to

make it alive. Dead nation? Yes! The fact that there is injustice in our country says that we are dead.

The fact there is racism and hate says we are dead.

The fact that people go to bed hungry at night says we are dead.

The fact that there are people who do not participate fully in the American way of life or in the democratic process says we are dead.

And God is asking, "Can America live again?"

We can only live as we stop trying to create revolutions that have no life and begin to have God breathe through us, to revive us.

Secondly, the Spirit of God came as fire. If wind speaks of the ability of God to take that which is dead and make it alive (regeneration), then fire speaks of purification. There are many people, who when they hear the word purity, misunderstand it. When they think of impurity, they think of socially immoral things and dirty people. Drunkards. Alcoholics. Murderers. Thieves. They think of impurity in that sense.

But when God talks about impurity, He is not talking only about that. He is talking about any situation where He is not functioning. Wherever God is *not* doing His thing, there is impurity. Purity is when God is burning His life through an individual, when an individual is making himself available to Jesus Christ and letting Christ live through him.

Essentially, Jesus said to His disciples, "It is necessary that I go away. Because if I don't go away the Spirit will not come. But when He is come, He will reprove the world of sin. He will convict the world of righteousness, because you won't see Me anymore." In other words, Christ was saying, "I am the personification of righteousness. If you want to know what purity is, I'm it." Then one of the disciples asked, "Lord, why don't You show us the Father, show us God so that we might be satisfied?" Jesus said, "Have you been so long with

Me and don't know that whoever has seen Me *has* seen the Father?"

Therefore, if Jesus Christ is our only standard of purity, an individual cannot become pure until he has the life of Christ flowing through him.

Moses was living on the back side of the desert for forty years. He was nothing more than his father-in-law's shepherd boy. And one day he saw a bush in the distance, burning but not being consumed. And when Moses turned aside to investigate the bush, God spoke to him. In essence He said, "Moses, don't get shook up about this bush. There is nothing really special about the bush. I can burn in the short, skinny bush next to you, the tall, fat one behind you, or the middle-sized one on your left. I can burn in any bush. The bush itself is not special. What makes the bush unique is that *I'm in it*."

And God is now saying, "I need human bushes. I need individuals in whom I can burn My life." God wants people today to be vehicles, instruments, bodies through which He can express Himself. God wants to take your life and burn through it — to purify you — to create in you a climate for His Spirit.

Thirdly, the Holy Spirit came as tongues. If wind speaks of regeneration and fire speaks of purification, then tongues speak of communication — the ability of God to communicate through people. This communication goes two ways. As these men were filled with the life of God, the whole new avenue of communicating to God took place. People learned how to talk to God and they learned how to listen to Him.

One of the great problems of our time is that many people do not really know how to talk to God. But when real revival takes place, when there is real spiritual awakening, people learn how to communicate to God. The barriers that separate you and God are torn down. There is a bridge that brings the two of you together so that you are on speaking terms.

Some of the people, when they hear the words prayer and communication, get shook up. They say, "I don't know how to pray." What they mean by that is that they have been listening to some religious people pray, and they say, "I can't pray like *that*." That used to be my hang-up. When I went to church these people would come up with this great articulate way of talking to God and I would sit there dumbfounded. I just couldn't pray like that. That wasn't my style. I came off the streets, you know, from the gangs, from the nitty-gritty. We didn't talk like that out in the streets. But I discovered God understands any way you talk to Him. You don't need to use "Thee," "Thou" and "Thou wouldst." The whole point is that you can talk naturally to God. You can sit down and talk with God in normal conversational tones, the way you would converse with anyone else. You don't have to use any special language, find any fancy words. You don't have to produce a special holy atmosphere. You could be taking a shower, washing the dishes, scrubbing the floor, or riding a bus — and you can talk to God. And God will understand you.

I am reminded of a former gang member, a young man from the streets of New York, who came to know Jesus Christ through a personal witness I gave him. Shortly after his conversion, he was walking in a particular neighborhood controlled by a gang he had fought against a few weeks before he committed himself to Christ. Of course, they had no way of knowing he had since left the gang. And when they saw him walking, the word spread quickly and before long a whole group of rival gang members started coming toward him. As he later related the situation, he told me, "Man, I walked across the street and I saw them dudes comin' after me. So I quick turned up my head and talked to the Big Cat upstairs. I asked Him to get me out of this bag and right quick!"

Now there are some church people who would say he was being irreverent. They think he should have stopped in the middle of the street and prayed, "O Thou Almighty God, Thou dost see mine enemy coming after me. . . ."

No way! God knew what he was saying. He didn't have to change his language to get through to God.

Unfortunately, many of us who talk in the church are talking only to ourselves. And there are some people who, when they get up to pray, are not praying to God, they're praying to *people,* trying to impress others.

When a person gets turned on by God, not only does he talk to God in normal conversational language, he learns to listen to what God says to him. Men talk to God, but don't forget God *speaks* to men as well. These early apostles heard Him and responded by taking His words to others.

The communication also went out to people. One of the great problems of our time is that the church is not talking to the world in language that the world understands. People come to some of our church services on Sunday morning and can't understand a thing that is going on. Our style, our language, customs and ways are alien to people who have no church affiliation. We must learn to begin to communicate who Jesus Christ is in language the world can understand.

I went on a retreat with a friend of mine who is a chaplain of a prison in Ohio. Once a year he takes a group of trusted prisoners out for a weekend meeting. At the close of this retreat we were gathered around the campfire and we asked those inmates who wanted to pray, or give a word of testimony about what the weekend had meant to them, to get up and speak. So one by one they stood and spoke briefly. Finally, one fellow got up, closed his eyes and lifted his head to heaven and said. "Lord, I want to thank You. I've had one helluva time!"

Now if he would have said that in church we would have thrown him out. But God understood what he was saying. The important thing is what a man is saying in his heart. Is his attitude right? If a man's attitude is right and his worship is right, God understands what he's saying.

We must also learn to communicate in language people understand. People outside the church don't understand us because we're not talking their language. We must somehow begin to communicate to the world. This was the original mission of the church. But how we've strayed!

Now I want you to understand, I'm not against the church. I'm a minister of the Gospel, which means I am part of the church. I am committed to the church. But because of my commitment to the church and my understanding of what the churches ought to be, I'm telling you that we have to get out of what we've become and return to what the New Testament calls church.

You see, the church is called the *ecclesia,* "a called-out people." *God has called us out to send us in.* It is the responsibility of the church to go into the world to *change the world.*

You can't change the world by isolating yourself from it or by withdrawing from it. Jesus said, "Go ye, therefore, into all the world." Not just the cloistered walls of our churches, not just 11:00 o'clock Sunday morning. The mission of the church, after it meets together for worship, is to go out and shake the world. We are to go "into the hedges and byways," not always in the respectable places. I'm talking about the hedges and byways — the red-light district, skid row, where the prostitutes, drunks and drug addicts are. That's where the church is supposed to be. And that's where Jesus went. He went out and rubbed shoulders with these unsavory people. The greatest accusation brought against Jesus Christ is that "this man eateth and drinketh with sinners." The religious crowd who were too stuck-up and too self-righteous to have anything to do with those people, wanted to have Him crucified for doing so.

There are people in the church who say, "But we can't go out there. We can't go out and rub shoulders with those kind of people. We might lose our testimony."

What?

How in all the world can you *lose your testimony* if you're going out to *share it?*

What they really mean is this: "If I go to those places and am seen talking with people of ill repute, people might condemn me. I might lose my testimony."

They're really afraid of a bunch of narrow-minded, big-oted, self-righteous, close-minded people who call themselves Christians. Well, why are you worried about *them?* They claim to be Christians already. Don't concern yourself about them! The church has to go to people who *need* God's help. Remember Jesus said, "Those who are well don't need a physician."

Physicians are for sick people. You have to go out into a sick world, sit down and relate to sick people, to frustrated people, to alcoholic people, to emotionally ill people, to drug addicts. You have to relate to racketeers and street gangs. You have to go to the places where our young people are hanging out, trying to find answers to their questions and problems and relating to them in the name of Jesus. That's where the church *has* to go if it is to survive. But some of us are a little too holy to get a little smoke blown into our faces. We're too pious to rub shoulders with a smelly drunk. Some of us act as if we have virgin ears and can't listen to their language.

And yet we claim to be the "salt of the earth." Salt goes on something you want to preserve. If you want to "preserve" people, go out and pour yourself out on them. That's where the church is supposed to be.

The church ought to be like a football huddle. Those of

you who understand the rules of football know they only allow you to stay in the huddle for twenty-five seconds. If you stay longer, you're penalized five yards for delay of the game. The reason is they want you to spend the majority of the time playing the game. So what's the job of the huddle? To call the next play — it's the strategy meeting. The quarterback brings the team into the huddle and says, "All right, we're going to run 44 on two." And they break. "44 on two" might mean that on the second count, the center will hand the ball to the quarterback who will hand off to the left halfback, who will carry the ball off right tackle. When that happens, every man knows what he's supposed to do. The right guard will pull out and try to block the left end, the right tackle will block the left guard, the right end will block the left tackle, the left guard will pull out and block the right linebacker, and the center will block the left linebacker. Every man knows what he's supposed to do. They all work like a team to make that play work. And when the play is over they might get five yards, ten yards, or might score a touchdown. But whatever happens, they come back to the huddle and call the strategy for the next play.

The huddle is merely the place where you call the strategy. You don't spend all the time in the huddle. You just come together for planning your next action. The problem with the church today is that we spend all our time in the huddle and never get out to play the game. That's why many think that serving the Lord is simply participating in the organizational structure of the church program.

"Are you serving the Lord?"

"Sure, I'm serving the Lord. I'm the president of the *Uncloudy Day Club* in my church."

"Yeah? What do you do?"

"Well, we put on programs and raise money."

They think serving the Lord is putting on programs to raise money. Anyone can do that!

That's not church, though. Church is going out into the world. And when that happens, revival comes. If the church is going to be relevant to the twentieth century, it has to get up off its seat, stop spending all of its time in the huddle, cloistering around itself, and go out to confront a world that's dying, a world that's sick, a world that needs help.

Jesus Christ set the standard. He illustrated this point when a group of people came to Him for entrance into the kingdom. He told them to depart from Him.

And they said, "But why, Lord?"

In essence He answered, "Simple. When I was hungry, you didn't give Me any meat. When I was thirsty, you didn't give Me any drink. When I was naked, you didn't clothe Me. When I was in prison, you didn't visit Me."

"But Lord, when did we see You in that condition? I mean, Lord, if we had seen You, we'd have helped You out."

But how can you see Christ in that condition if all your time is spent in the church building? You can't see Jesus until you get out into the world where people are in need — because those are the ones with whom He associates.

The church should be the place where God's people come together to worship God and be built up in the faith. The church is also the place for fellowship. God's people share with one another their lives, their weaknesses, their triumphs and grievances. They weep with one another, they suffer with one another. They pray each other through. They help one another. That's what real fellowship is. But most of us think that fellowship is building a special hall next to the sanctuary dubbed "Fellowship Hall," constructed especially for "a time of fellowship." Namely, tea, coffee and cookies. And we call that fellowship.

Genuine Christian fellowship is where people are committed to one another, looking out for the welfare of one another.

Do you realize that the city of Chicago is the "most

churched" city in all of America? Yet with all of the churches, church organizations and rescue missions, Chicago is one of the most explosive, the most divided cities in America. People are not together because the church is not out there bringing them together.

We have to go out where the world is. That's the secret given to believers at this occasion — "Go ye into all the world, and preach My Gospel," Jesus is saying.

Men came to the disciples and asked them what was going on. They said, "Are these men drunk?"

Peter said, "They *are* intoxicated, but not drunk with wine."

The word intoxicated doesn't mean that they were staggering around the streets like fools. The word *intoxicated* means "to be under the influence of." These men were *under the influence* of the *Holy Spirit*. They were intoxicated by God. And under His influence, Peter explained what was happening. He said, "This is what the prophet Joel spoke about when he said, 'God says, in the last days I will pour out my spirit upon all flesh. And young men shall have visions and old men shall dream dreams.' "

When revival takes place in our society and in the church, *young men will have visions*. One of the great blights on the church today is that most of our young people aren't even there to have these visions — they are copping out on church, some with justifiable reasons. Often we are not making the message of Jesus Christ relevant to this generation. Did you realize that the average age in the United States right now is about twenty-five? The majority of the people alive in our country have been born since 1945. But let's look at our churches and ask ourselves the average age of our church members. In some of our churches we are thirty years older than the national average.

If your church is typical, do you know the average age of people living around your church? It's twenty-five years old.

Is that the average age in your church?

When revival comes, it ought to be bringing into the church young people who have vision and idealistic energy, who in the name of Jesus want to go out and shake up the world.

There are some of us young people committed to changing the world. We're committed to changing the system. We're not going to leave the world the way we found it.

The church should have the mission to take this drive, this energy, this idealism of young people, and get them plugged in to God. While in this "huddle" the church should teach them the relevancy of the Gospel and send them back out in the name of God to shake the world.

But our problem is that there are many older church leaders who aren't prepared to let young people move. "I've been playing this piano for the last thirty-five years and I'm going to stay here. I've got seniority!"

Instead of this, when there is real revival in the church, there should also be the development of young people. Old people should say to young people, "Look. I can't run around like I used to, but in these few years that I've been plugged in to God, I've learned a couple of things and I'd like to pass on my experience to you young people." If you combine your experiences with their energy and idealism and send them out into the world to do the job, you'll see revival!

The apostle Paul said you are not operating properly unless you are producing leaders. If you are a Sunday school teacher, have you trained someone to take your place? Have you poured yourself into a younger person who can stand up and teach that class as well, if not better than you can, because *you* taught them?

If you are the pastor of a church, is there someone in your church whom you have trained, ready to take your place if needed right now?

Corruption is generated in churches because of selfish religious leaders who haven't learned the basic principles of leadership. Industry has learned long ago that the job of a leader is to pour himself into other people who can replace him. And in the process the teacher becomes even more valuable and experienced.

In the attempt to protect ourselves, however, we hold on to our power until we move away or die. Then people start fighting for our job. You are not a successful pastor until you are pouring yourself into younger men. Your church shouldn't have to go around the country looking for candidates to take your place. You can have several young men prepared to come up and replace you if something happens. That's the mission of the church. Young men should have visions and old men should dream dreams.

How did all of this happen? They asked Peter, "How is all of this happening? How are these people filled with the Spirit?"

Peter answered, in essence, that the Holy Spirit is poured out because Christ is exalted. You cannot be filled with the life of Jesus until you let Him be exalted in your life. The word "exalted" means to let Him be Lord. Let Him run your life. The New Testament records an instance where those around Jesus were thirsty. He stood up and said, "If any man thirst, let him come to Me and drink. And out of his innermost being will flow rivers of living water." And the apostle John wrote, "This spake he of the Holy Spirit which was not yet given because Christ was not yet exalted."

But now Peter is saying in essence, *"Christ is exalted.* Christ is now at the right hand of His Father, above all principalities and powers. And because He is Lord and we have received Him as Lord, He has filled us with Himself and has sent us out into the streets of Jerusalem to bring about a revolution in the name of God."

If you want to know what it means then to be Christian, you want to learn what it means to be filled with the life of

Christ; if you want Jesus Christ to run your life, let Him be exalted. Give Him your all. Let Him be Lord in your life, to run your life. Is that what you want?

I don't care what you say about how the world needs to be changed. You can't change it until you begin with yourself. If you want to radicalize the world, if you want to radicalize your church, if you want to see things changed, you must begin with a change in yourself. Come to Christ and let Him live His life through you. You can be a statesman for God; you can pour yourself into younger men and women who will go out in the name of Jesus to radicalize a system that needs to be brought down.

But the system can only be brought down on a basis of justice, love and mercy. And that kind of living fruit cannot come from dead people. It must come from people who are alive. Now if that's what you want, then I invite you to pray, "Lord Jesus Christ, I want You to be Lord of my life. I want You to run my life. I want to be Christian in the fullest sense of the term. I want to be awakened. I want to be revived. I want to be part of the Church. I want Jesus Christ to live in me. Lord Jesus, come into me right now and take over my life.

Let the revolution begin with me!"

Tom Skinner Associates is engaged in communicating the same transforming message that changed Tom Skinner's life, to everyone in general and to black people in particular. If you would like to have more information please write:

Tom Skinner Associates, Inc.
521 Hopkinson Avenue
Brooklyn, New York 11212
Area Code 212   498-1717